ACCA

Strategic Business Reporting (SBR (INT/UK))

Pocket Notes

British library cataloguing-in-publication data

A catalogue record for this book is available from the British Library.

Published by:
Kaplan Publishing UK
Unit 2 The Business Centre
Molly Millars Lane
Wokingham
Berkshire
RG41 2QZ

ISBN 978-1-83996-175-5

Printed and bound in Great Britain.

Acknowledgements

This product contains copyright material and trademarks of the IFRS Foundation®. All rights reserved. Used under licence from the IFRS Foundation®. Reproduction and use rights are strictly limited. For more information about the IFRS Foundation and rights to use its material please visit www.ifrs.org.

Trade Marks

The Foundation has trade marks registered around the world ('**Trade Marks**') including 'IAS®', 'IASB®', 'IFRIC®', 'IFRS®', the IFRS® logo, 'IFRS for SMEs®', IFRS for SMEs® logo, the 'Hexagon Device', 'International Financial Reporting Standards®', NIIF® and 'SIC®'.

Further details of the Foundation's Trade Marks are available from the Licensor on request.

Contents

Chapter 1 Frameworks ... 1
Chapter 2 The professional and ethical duty of the accountant ... 9
Chapter 3 Performance reporting ... 15
Chapter 4 Revenue ... 23
Chapter 5 Non-current assets ... 29
Chapter 6 Agriculture and inventories ... 41
Chapter 7 Foreign currency in individual financial statements ... 43
Chapter 8 Leases ... 47
Chapter 9 Employee benefits ... 55
Chapter 10 Share-based payment ... 63
Chapter 11 Provisions and events after the reporting period ... 69
Chapter 12 Financial instruments ... 75
Chapter 13 Tax ... 89
Chapter 14 Segment reporting ... 95

Chapter 15 Related parties 99

Chapter 16 Adoption of International Financial Reporting Standards 103

Chapter 17 Small and medium entities 107

Chapter 18 Group accounting – basic groups 113

Chapter 19 Change in group structure 129

Chapter 20 Group accounting – foreign currency 135

Chapter 21 Group statement of cash flows 141

Chapter 22 Analysis and interpretation 147

Chapter 23: Current issues 157

Chapter 24: UK GAAP 167

References R.1

Index I.1

This document references IFRS® Standards and IAS® Standards, which are authored by the International Accounting Standards Board (the Board), and published in the 2021 IFRS Standards Red Book.

The exam

Paper background

The exam requires students to examine corporate reporting from a number of perspectives. Students will be required to assess and evaluate reporting decisions made by management, their implications for a range of stakeholders, and the professional and ethical issues raised. Students are expected to be able to prepare and discuss consolidated financial statements. Knowledge of current issues in corporate reporting is also required.

Exam format

The exam is three hours and fifteen minutes. All questions are compulsory.

Section A (50%) consists of two scenario based questions. The first questions will be based on financial statements of group entities. The second question will require consideration of the reporting and ethical implications of specific events.

Section B (50%) consists of two questions. These may be scenario or case-study or essay-based and could deal with any part of the syllabus. Section B will always include a full question or a part of a question that tests the interpretation section of the syllabus.

UK syllabus

UK syllabus students sit an exam that is almost identical to the International syllabus exam. In the UK exam, Section B questions will be adapted to test UK specific content for approximately 15-20 marks. This content is covered in Chapter 24.

Keys to success in SBR

- Read widely
- Study the whole syllabus
- Do not neglect the 'softer' topics – analysis and current issues are core parts of the syllabus
- Manage your time carefully to ensure that you finish the paper
- Knowledge of the accounting standards is not enough. You must be able to apply the standards to unfamiliar scenarios
- Practice exam questions to time.

Quality and accuracy are of the utmost importance to us so if you spot an error in any of our products, please send an email to mykaplanreporting@kaplan.com with full details, or follow the link to the feedback form in MyKaplan.

Our Quality Co-ordinator will work with our technical team to verify the error and take action to ensure it is corrected in future editions.

chapter

1

Frameworks

In this chapter

- Conceptual Framework.
- IFRS 13 Fair Value Measurement.

The Conceptual Framework

Exam focus

The Conceptual Framework is an important topic in SBR. You should expect it to feature in every exam.

Purposes

The key purposes of the Conceptual Framework are to assist:

- the Board when developing new IFRS Standards
- preparers of financial statements when no IFRS Standard applies to a transaction, or when an IFRS Standard offers a choice of accounting policy
- all parties when understanding and interpreting IFRS Standards.

The purpose of financial reporting

The purpose of financial reporting is to provide information to current and potential investors, lenders and other creditors that will enable them to make decisions about providing economic resources to an entity.

User groups need information to assess:

- an entity's potential future cash flows, and
- management's stewardship of the entity's economic resources.

This information is provided in financial statements.

Qualitative characteristics

Key Point

Financial information is only useful if it embodies the fundamental characteristics.

The enhancing characteristics make financial information more useful.

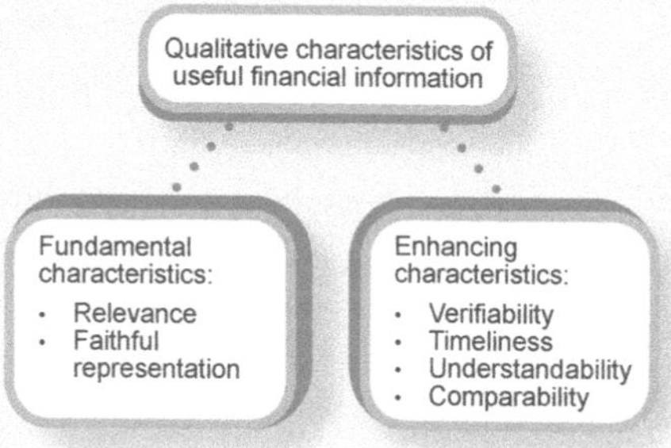

Qualitative characteristics of useful financial information

Fundamental characteristics:

- Relevance
- Faithful representation

Enhancing characteristics:

- Verifiability
- Timeliness
- Understandability
- Comparability

The elements

Definition

The elements are the building blocks of financial statements.

An economic resource is a **'right that has the potential to produce economic benefits'** (para 4.4).

Asset	**'A present economic resource controlled by an entity as a result of a past event'** (para 4.3)
Liability	**'A present obligation of the entity to transfer an economic resource as a result of a past event'** (para 4.26).
Equity	The residual interest in the net assets of an entity.
Income	Increases in assets or decreases in liabilities that result in an increase to equity (excluding contributions from equity holders).
Expenses	Decreases in assets or increases in liabilities that result in decreases to equity (excluding distributions to equity holders).

Recognition

Items are recognised in financial statements if:

- they meet the definition of an element, and
- recognition provides relevant information, and
- recognition faithfully represents the entity's financial performance and position.

Derecognition

Derecognition from financial statements normally occurs when the entity:

- loses control of the asset, or
- has no present obligation for the liability.

Accounting for derecognition should faithfully represent the changes in an entity's net assets, as well as any assets or liabilities retained. This involves:

- derecognising any transferred, expired or consumed component, and
- recognising a gain or loss on the above, and
- recognising any retained component.

Measurement

If recognised in the financial statements, an element must be quantified.

The Conceptual Framework outlines two measurement bases:

- historical cost
- current value (this includes fair value, value-in-use, and current cost).

When selecting a measurement basis, relevance is maximised if the following are considered:

- the characteristics of the asset or liability
- how the asset or liability contributes to future cash flows.

Presentation and disclosure

The statement of profit or loss is the primary source of information about an entity's financial performance. Income and expenses should normally be recognised in this statement.

The Board might require an income or expense to be presented in other comprehensive income if it results from remeasuring an item to current value and if this means that:

- profit or loss provides more relevant information, or
- a more faithful representation is provided of an entity's performance.

Income and expenditure included in other comprehensive income should be reclassified to profit or loss when doing so results in profit or loss providing more relevant information.

IFRS 13 Fair Value Measurement

Definition

Fair value is defined as '**the price that would be received to sell an asset or paid to transfer a liability in an orderly transaction between market participants at the measurement date**' (IFRS 13, para 9).

Fair value hierarchy

Level 1 inputs

- Quoted prices for identical assets in active markets

Level 2 inputs

- Quoted prices for identical assets in less active markets
- Quoted prices for similar assets in active markets

Level 3 inputs

- Unobservable inputs

Priority is given to level 1 inputs when determining fair value.

Markets

Key Point

IFRS 13 says that fair value should be determined by reference to the principal market.

This is the market with the greatest volume of activity.

If the principal market cannot be determined then fair value should be measured based on the price in the most advantageous market.

Non-financial assets

Non-financial assets include:

- Property, plant and equipment
- Intangible assets

The fair value of a non-financial asset should be based on its **highest and best use.**

Exam focus

Exam Kit questions in this area

- Skizer
- Mehran
- Klancet
- Sitka

chapter

2

The professional and ethical duty of the accountant

In this chapter

- Overview.
- Ethical issues facing the accountant.
- Ethical codes of conduct.
- Consequences of unethical behaviour.

Overview

Exam focus

Question 2 in the SBR exam will test the reporting and ethical implications of specific events. Two professional marks will be awarded in this question.

Ethical issues facing the accountant

Definition

Professional ethics are the principles and standards that underlie the responsibilities and conduct of a person in performing his/ her function in a particular field of expertise.

- Ethical principles are important in a business organisation as they set the tone for the culture and behaviour of employees and management.
- The application of ethics can sometimes be intangible. Ethics is often described as 'doing the right thing' but this can mean different things to different individuals.

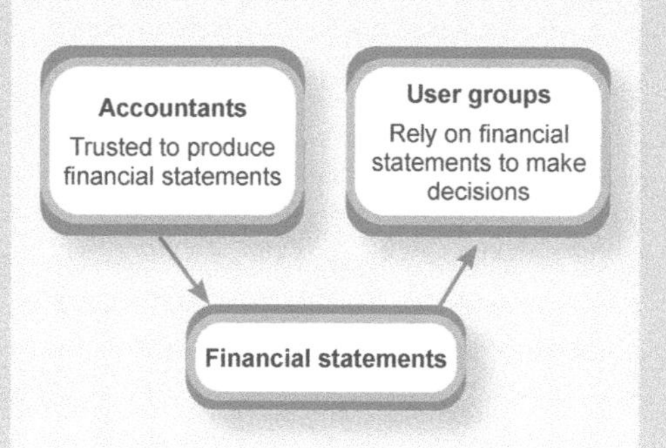

Ethical codes of conduct

Professional accountants are bound by their Institute or Association's codes of ethics and are expected to act in accordance with such codes of conduct.

ACCA Code of Ethics

The ACCA Code of Ethics and Conduct applies to all students, associates and members. The Code is in the form of a framework and adopts a principles-based approach; whilst some specific rules are included, compliance is largely concerned with the observation of the fundamental principles.

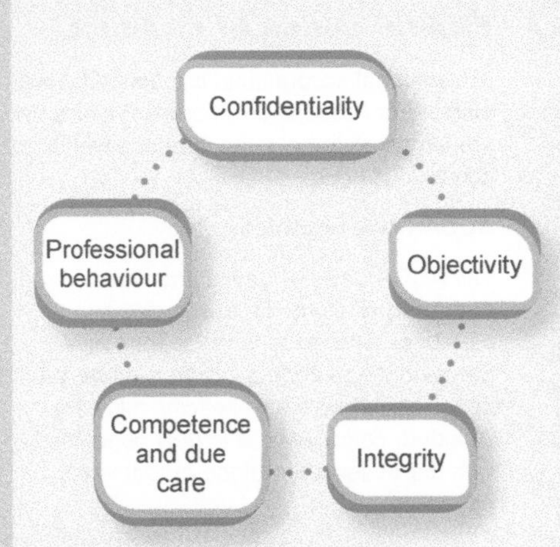

- **Integrity** – Members should be straightforward and honest in all professional and business relationships.
- **Objectivity** – Members should not allow bias, conflicts of interest or undue influence of others to override their judgement.
- **Professional competence and due care** – Members have a continuing duty to maintain professional knowledge and skill at a level required to ensure that a client or employer receives a competent and professional service.
- **Confidentiality** – Members should respect the confidentiality of information acquired as a result of professional and business relationships and should not disclose any such information to third parties without proper and specific authority.
- **Professional behaviour** – Members should comply with relevant laws and regulations and avoid any action that discredits the profession.

Consequences of unethical behaviour

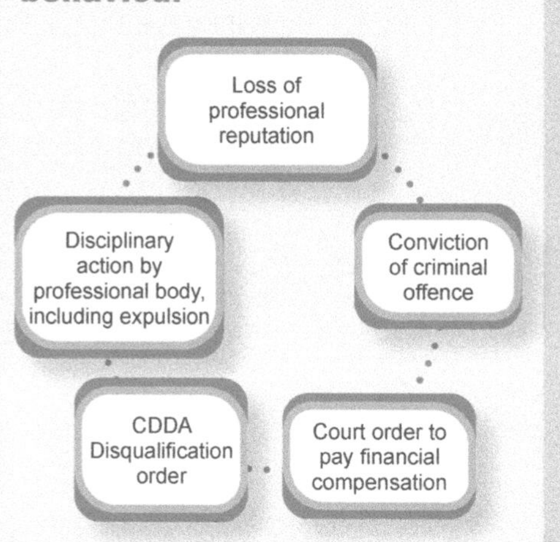

Exam focus

Exam Kit questions in this area:

- Calibra
- Stent
- Hudson
- Fiskerton
- Bismuth
- Agency Group

chapter

3

Performance reporting

In this chapter

- Overview.
- IAS 1 Presentation of financial statements.
- Accounting concepts to apply in preparation of financial statements.
- IAS 8 Accounting policies, changes in accounting estimates and errors.
- IFRS 5 Non-current assets held for sale and discontinued operations.
- IAS 34 Interim Financial Reporting.

Overview

Exam focus

- Many of these accounting standards were covered in your previous studies.
- The level of application required in this exam will be much higher.

IAS 1 Presentation of Financial Statements

IAS 1 provides recommended formats for the statement of profit or loss and other comprehensive income, the statement of financial position, and the statement of changes in equity. It also details issues to be included in disclosure notes.

Statement of financial position

Assets and liabilities must be classified as current or non-current.

Definition

A current asset is an asset that:

- will be realised or consumed during the entity's normal trading cycle, or
- is held for trading, or
- will be realised within 12 months of the reporting date.

A current liability is a liability that:

- will be settled during the entity's normal trading cycle, or
- is held for trading, or
- will be settled within 12 months of the reporting date.
- the entity does not have the right as at the reporting date to defer settlement beyond 12 months.

Profit or loss and other comprehensive income (OCI)

According to the Conceptual Framework, profit or loss is the primary source of information about an entity's financial performance during the period.

OCI are income and expenses that, in accordance with IFRS Standards, are recognised outside of profit or loss.

Items of OCI must be presented as either:

- items that might be reclassified to profit or loss in the future
- items that will not be reclassified to profit or loss in the future.

Disclosure notes

Disclosure notes supplement the primary financial statements. They include important information about:

- material accounting policies
- sources of uncertainty
- valuation and estimation techniques
- unrecognised items (such as contingent liabilities)
- events after the reporting period.

Disclosure notes should be ordered systematically. This might mean:

- displaying the most relevant issues prominently
- grouping similar items together
- following the order in which items are presented in the primary financial statements.

Accounting concepts to apply in preparation of financial statements

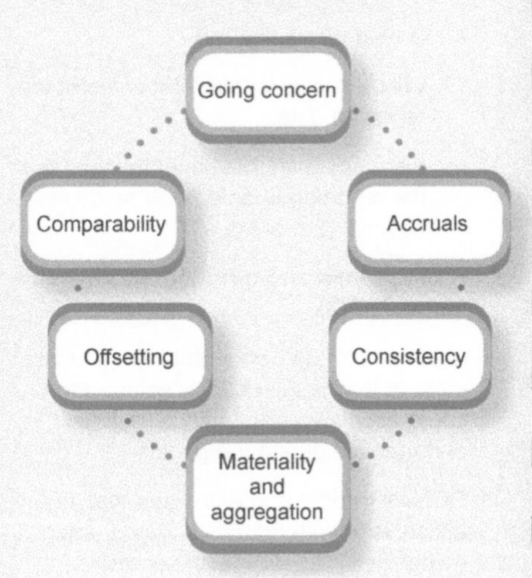

IAS 8 Accounting policies, changes in accounting estimates and errors

Selecting accounting policies

Accounting policies must be determined by applying the relevant IFRS Standard. If there is no standard, then management should choose an accounting policy that results in relevant and reliable financial information.

Changing accounting policies

Accounting policies can only change if:

- the change is required by a standard or interpretation; or
- the change results in more relevant and reliable information.

Changes in accounting policies are accounted for retrospectively as if the new policy had always been applied.

Accounting Estimates

Accounting estimates are amounts that are subject to measurement uncertainty, such as:

- the measurement of a warranty provision
- depreciation of property, plant and equipment during the reporting period.

Changes in accounting estimates are accounted for prospectively.

Errors

Prior period errors are misstatements due to mistakes in applying accounting policies and fraud. They are corrected retrospectively.

IFRS 5 Non-current Assets Held for Sale and Discontinued Operations

Definition

Per IFRS 5, a discontinued operation is a component of an entity that has been sold, or which is classified as held for sale, and which is

- a separate line of business, or
- part of a plan to dispose of a separate line of business, or
- a subsidiary acquired solely for resale.

Presentation

A **single amount** for discontinued operations is presented on the face of the statement of profit or loss. This comprises:

- the post-tax profit or loss of the operation
- any profit or loss on disposal, or any loss on classification as held for sale.

Example statement of profit or loss showing discontinued operation

	20X2	20X1
	$m	$m
Revenue	200	190
Operating expenses	(40)	(50)
Finance cost	(20)	(20)
Profit before tax	140	120
Income tax expense	(30)	(25)
Profit from continuing operations	110	95
Discontinued operations		
Loss from discontinued operations*	(70)	(50)
Profit for the period	40	45

IAS 34 Interim Financial Reporting

Definition

An interim period '**is a financial reporting period that is shorter than a full financial year**' (IAS 34, para 4).

IAS 34 outlines the minimum content that should be included in an interim financial report.

The minimum content to be included is:

- A condensed statement of financial position
- A condensed statement of profit or loss and other comprehensive income
- A condensed statement of changes in equity
- A condensed statement of cash flows
- Selected disclosure notes.

Exam Focus

Exam Kit questions in this area:

- Moyes part (c)
- Traveler part (b)

chapter

4

Revenue

In this chapter

- Revenue recognition.
- Identify the contract.
- Identify the performance obligations.
- Determine the transaction price.
- Allocate the transaction price.
- Recognise revenue.
- Contract costs.

Revenue recognition

IFRS 15 Revenue from Contracts with Customers adopts a five step approach to revenue recognition:

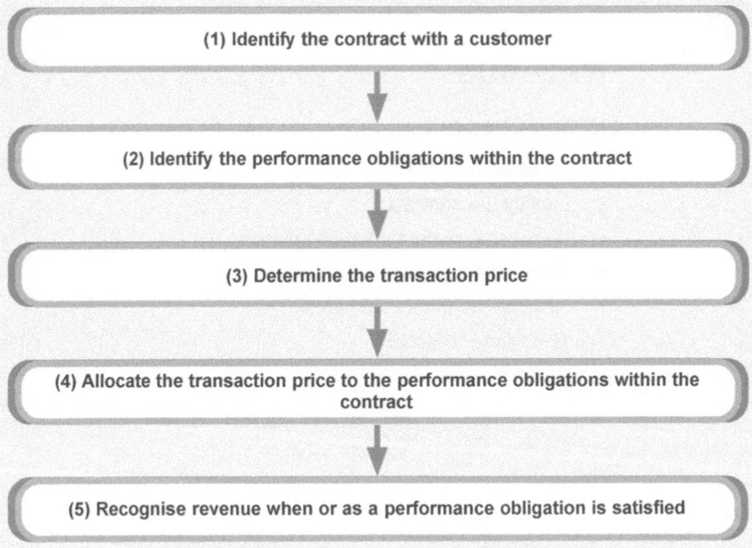

Identify the contract

IFRS 15 Revenue from Contracts with Customers says that a contract is an agreement between two parties that creates rights and obligations.

An entity can only account for revenue from a contract if it meets the following criteria:

- the parties have approved the contract and each party's rights can be identified
- payment terms can be identified
- the contract has commercial substance
- it is probable that the selling entity will receive consideration.

Identify the performance obligations

The distinct performance obligations within a contract must be identified.

Definition

Performance obligations are promises to transfer distinct goods or services to a customer.

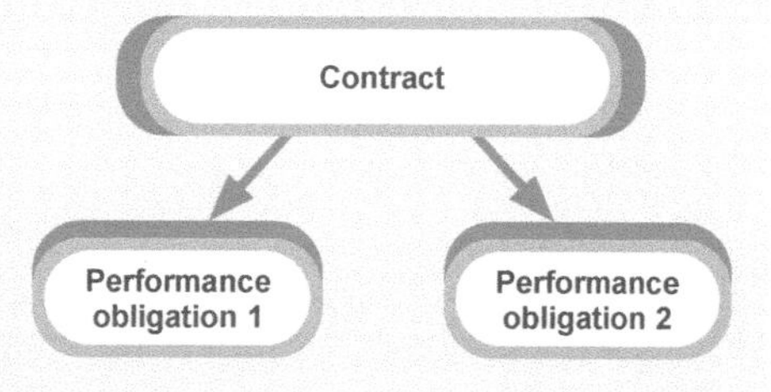

Entities must determine the nature of their performance obligation. They might be:

- a **principal** (providing the good or service)
- an **agent** (arranging for the good or service to be provided by another party).

An entity is the principal if it controls the good or service before it is transferred to the buyer.

Determine the transaction price

Definition

The transaction price is the consideration that the selling entity will be entitled to once it has fulfilled the performance obligations in the contract

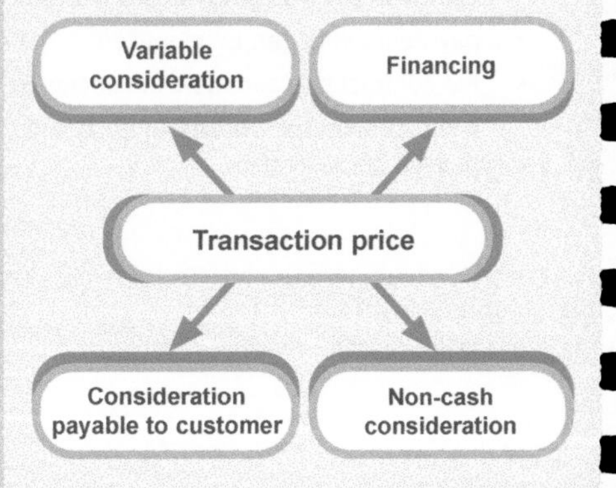

Variable consideration (i.e. a bonus or a penalty)

The seller must estimate the amount expected to be received.

This estimate is included in the transaction price if it is **highly probable** that a **significant reversal in the amount of revenue recognised will not occur** when the uncertainty is resolved.

Financing

If there is a significant financing component, the consideration receivable must be discounted to present value.

Non-cash consideration

This is measured at fair value.

Consideration payable to a customer

This is deducted from the transaction price.

Allocate the transaction price

Key Point

The total transaction price should be allocated to each performance obligation in proportion to standalone selling prices.

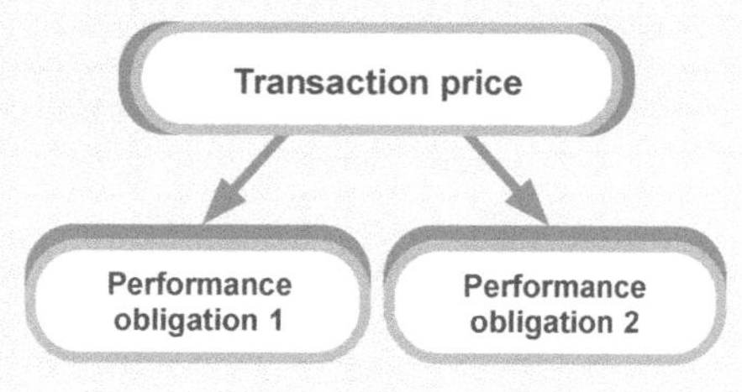

Recognise revenue

Key Point

Revenue is recognised when (or as) the entity satisfies a performance obligation.

An entity only satisfies a performance obligation over time if one of the following criteria is met:

- the customer simultaneously receives and consumes the benefits from the entity's performance as it performs
- the entity is creating or enhancing an asset controlled by the customer
- the entity cannot use the asset 'for an alternative use' and the entity can demand payment for its performance to date.

If a performance obligation is **satisfied over time**, then revenue is recognised based on the progress towards completion.

If a performance obligation is not satisfied over time then it is satisfied at **a point in time**. This is normally when the customer **obtains control** of the promised asset.

Contract costs

An entity must capitalise:

- the costs of obtaining a contract
- the costs of fulfilling a contract that do not fall within the scope of another standard (such as IAS 2 Inventories)

Exam focus

Exam Kit questions in this area include:

- Zedtech
- Carsoon
- Verge
- Sitka

chapter

5

Non-current assets

In this chapter

- Overview.
- IAS 16 Property, plant and equipment.
- IAS 20 Accounting for government grants and disclosure of government assistance.
- IAS 23 Borrowing costs.
- IAS 40 Investment property.
- IAS 38 Intangible assets.
- IAS 36 Impairment of assets.
- IFRS 5 Non-current assets held for sale.

Overview

Exam focus

- This chapter focuses on standards relating to tangible and intangible assets.
- All of these have been studied previously but are regularly examined.
- This chapter is a reminder of the key points.

IAS 16 Property, plant and equipment

Key Point

Property, plant and equipment is initially recognised at cost.

Subsequent expenditure on non-current assets may be capitalised if it:

- enhances the economic benefits of the asset, e.g. adding a new wing to a building
- replaces part of an asset that has been separately depreciated, and has been fully depreciated e.g. a furnace that requires new linings
- replaces economic benefits previously consumed, e.g. a major inspection of aircraft.

The asset is depreciated over its useful life.

- The **depreciation method** and **useful life** of an asset should be reviewed at the end of each year.
- If an asset has parts with **different lives**, (e.g. a building with a flat roof), the component parts of the asset should be depreciated separately.

Revaluation of property, plant and equipment

Revaluation to fair value is **optional**. If one asset is revalued, all assets in that class must be revalued.

- Revaluation **gains** are credited to other comprehensive income unless the gain reverses a previous revaluation loss of the same asset previously recognised in profit or loss.
- Revaluation **losses** are charged to the statement of profit or loss unless the loss relates to a previous revaluation surplus, in which case it should be charged to other comprehensive income.
- The revised carrying amount is depreciated over the remaining useful life of the asset.
- An entity may choose to make a **reserves transfer** for the **excess depreciation** arising from a revaluation. This is taken from the revaluation reserve to retained earnings.

IAS 20 Accounting for government grants and disclosure of government assistance

Key Point

Grants should not be recognised until there is reasonable assurance that the grant will be received and that conditions will be complied with.

- Income grants given to subsidise expenditure should be matched to the related costs.
- Grants for purchases of non-current assets should be recognised over the expected useful lives of the related assets. There are two acceptable accounting policies for this:
  - deduct the grant from the cost of the asset and depreciate the net cost; or
  - treat the grant as deferred income and release to the statement of profit or loss over the life of the asset.

IAS 23 Borrowing costs

Definition

Borrowing costs are interest and other costs incurred when borrowing funds.

Entities **must capitalise** borrowing costs that are directly attributable to the acquisition, construction or production of assets that take a substantial amount of time to get ready for use.

IAS 40 Investment property

Definition

Investment property is property held to earn rentals or for capital appreciation or both.

Investment property is initially recognised at cost.

An entity can then choose either the **cost model** (cost less depreciation) or the **fair value model**.

- The **fair value model** recognises investment properties in the statement of financial position at **fair value**. **Gains** and **losses** on remeasurement are recognised in the **statement of profit or loss**.

IAS 38 Intangible assets

Definition

An **intangible asset 'is an identifiable non-monetary asset without physical substance**' (IAS 38, para 8).

- An intangible asset is initially recognised at cost if:

  (1) It is identifiable.

  (2) It is controlled by the entity.

  (3) It will generate probable future economic benefits for the entity.

  (4) The cost can be measured reliably.

- If an intangible does not meet the recognition criteria, then it should be charged to the statement of profit or loss as expenditure is incurred.

- Intangible assets should be amortised over their useful lives.

- If it can be demonstrated that the useful life is indefinite then no amortisation should be charged but an annual impairment review must be carried out.

- Intangible assets can be revalued but only if fair values can be determined with reference to an active market.

- Costs incurred during the research must be expensed as they are incurred. Costs incurred during development should be recognised as an asset if they meet the following criteria:

  (a) the project is technically feasible

  (b) the asset will be completed then used or sold

  (c) the entity is able to use or sell the asset

(d) the asset will generate future economic benefits

(e) the entity has adequate technical, financial and other resources to complete the project

(f) the expenditure on the project can be reliably measured.

- Amortisation over the useful life of the new product or process will commence once the project is complete.

IAS 36 Impairment of assets

Definition

An **impairment loss** is the amount by which the carrying amount of an asset or cash-generating unit exceeds its recoverable amount.

Impairment is measured by comparing the carrying amount of an asset with its recoverable amount.

Key Point

If the carrying amount exceeds the recoverable amount, the asset is impaired and must be written down.

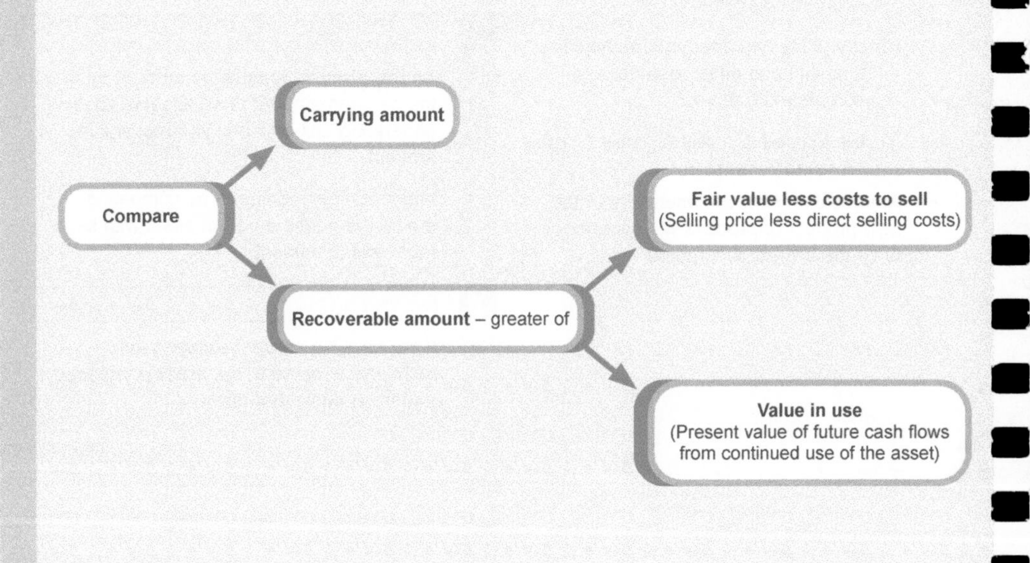
Carrying amount
Compare
Fair value less costs to sell
(Selling price less direct selling costs)
Recoverable amount – greater of
Value in use
(Present value of future cash flows
from continued use of the asset)

Indicators of impairment

Impairment reviews are required where there is an indicator of impairment.

Internal Indicators:

- Physical damage to the asset.
- Management committed to reorganisation of the business.
- Idle or obsolete assets.
- Operating losses in the business where the assets are used.

External Indicators:

- Competitor actions.
- Increasing interest rates (because this reduces the value in use).
- Market values of assets falling.

Cash-generating units (CGU)

Key Point

Individual assets may not generate a distinguishable cash flow. In this case the impairment calculation should be based on a CGU.

Definition

A **cash-generating unit** is the smallest group of assets that generates independent cash inflows.

Impairment losses on a CGU are allocated in the following order:

(1) goodwill

(2) remaining assets in proportion to carrying amounts.

No asset can be written down below the higher of fair value less costs to sell, value in use and zero.

Recognition of impairment losses

Assets held at cost: The amount of the impairment is charged to the statement of profit or loss.

Revalued assets: The impairment is charged to other comprehensive income to reverse any previous surplus on that asset with any excess charged to profit or loss.

IFRS 5 Non-current assets held for sale

Definition

An asset should be classified as held for sale if its carrying amount will be recovered principally through a sales transaction.

To be classified as held for sale, the following criteria must be met:

- The asset must be available for sale in its present condition
- The sale must be highly probable
- Management must be committed to the sale
- The asset should be actively marketed at a reasonable price
- The sale must be expected within a year.

If the criteria are met:

- The asset should be measured at the lower of carrying amount and fair value less costs to sell.
- If the asset is measured using a revaluation model then it should be revalued to fair value before being classified as held for sale.
- The asset will be presented as a current asset
- No further depreciation is charged.

Exam focus

Exam Kit questions in this area:

- Corbel
- Leria
- Skizer
- Emcee
- Bismuth
- Symbal
- Colat
- Agency Group

chapter

6

Agriculture and Inventories

In this chapter

- IAS 41 Agriculture.
- IAS 2 Inventories.

IAS 41 Agriculture

Definition

A biological asset is a '**living plant or animal**' (IAS 41, para 5).

Agricultural produce is the '**harvested product of the entity's biological assets**' (IAS 41, para 5).

The key rules from the standard are:

- Biological assets are initially measured at fair value less estimated costs to sell.
- At each reporting date, biological assets are revalued to fair value less costs to sell.
- At the date of harvest, agricultural produce should be recognised and measured at fair value less estimated costs to sell. It is then accounted for under IAS 2 Inventories.

IAS 2 Inventories

Definition

Inventories are assets that the entity sells in the ordinary course of business (plus any raw materials and work in progress).

Inventories are measured at '**the lower of cost and net realisable value**' (IAS 2, para 9):

- **Cost** includes the purchase price and any other directly attributable costs.
- **Net realisable value** is the expected selling price, less estimated costs of completion and sale.

Exam focus

Exam Kit questions in this area:

- Fill
- Lucky Dairy

chapter

7

Foreign currency in individual financial statements

In this chapter

- Functional currency.
- Translation rules.

Functional currency

Definition

IAS 21 The Effects of Changes in Foreign Exchange Rates states that functional currency is '**the currency of the primary economic environment where an entity operates**' (IAS 21, para 8).

Factors used to determine a functional currency are as follows:

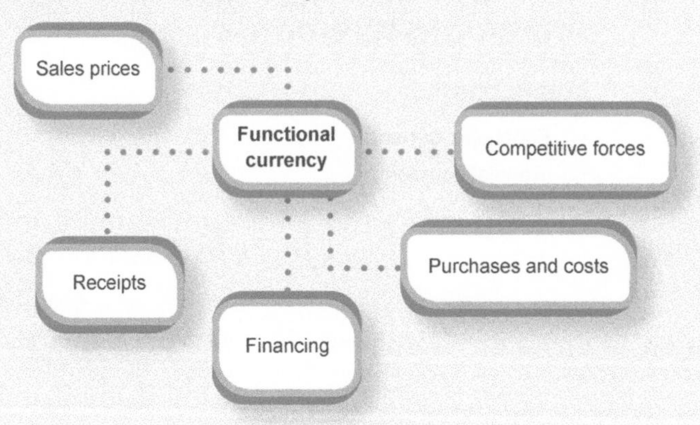

A subsidiary that operates with little autonomy will most likely have the same functional currency as its parent.

Translation rules

Overseas transactions

Initial transaction

Translate into functional currency using the spot/historic rate.

Settlement

Translate the settlement into functional currency using the spot/historic rate.

If unsettled

The treatment depends on whether the overseas item is monetary.

If monetary

E.g. receivables, payables, loans

Retranslate at the closing rate of exchange.

If non-monetary

E.g. PPE, inventories

Do not retranslate.

However, if held under a fair value model, the fair value will need to be translated when determined.

Exam Focus

Exam Kit questions in this area:

- Carbise part (a) (i)
- Artwright part (c)

chapter

8

Leases

In this chapter

- IFRS 16 Leases.
- Lessee accounting.
- Lessor accounting.
- Sale and leaseback.

IFRS 16 Leases

Definition

A **lease** is a contract that conveys the right to use an underlying asset for a period of time in exchange for consideration.

The **lessor** is the entity that provides the right-of-use asset and, in exchange, receives consideration.

The **lessee** is the entity that obtains use of the right-of-use asset and, in exchange, transfers consideration.

Identifying a lease

A contract contains a lease if it conveys the right to control the use of an identified asset for a period of time in exchange for consideration. For this to be the case, the contract must give the customer:

- the right to substantially all of the economic benefits from use of the identified asset, and
- the right to direct the use of the identified asset

Lessee accounting

Initial treatment

Except for the exceptions noted later, the lessee should recognise a lease liability and a right-of-use asset at the commencement of the lease:

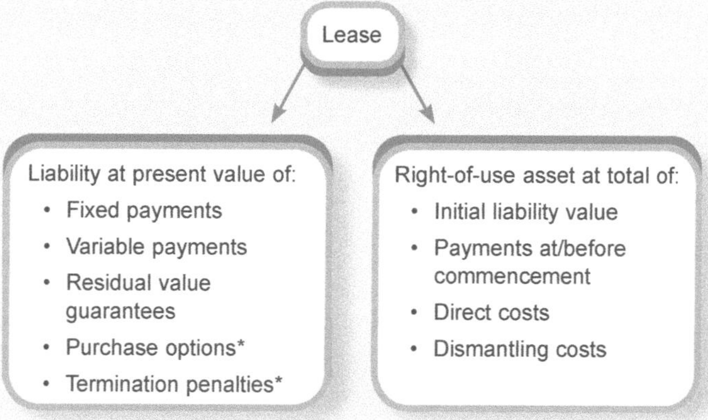

Lease

Liability at present value of:

- Fixed payments
- Variable payments
- Residual value guarantees
- Purchase options*
- Termination penalties*

Right-of-use asset at total of:

- Initial liability value
- Payments at/before commencement
- Direct costs
- Dismantling costs

* Include if reasonably certain to be incurred

Subsequent treatment

- The carrying amount of the lease liability is increased by the interest charge. This interest is also recorded in the statement of profit or loss. The carrying amount of the lease liability is reduced by cash repayments.
- The right-of-use asset is measured using the cost model (unless another measurement model is chosen). This means it is measured at its initial cost less accumulated depreciation and impairment losses.

Exceptions

The lessee can choose to recognise the lease payments in profit or loss on a straight line basis if the lease is

- short-term (less than 12 months at the inception date), or
- of a low value.

Lessor accounting

Lease classifications

Leases must be classified at inception as either a finance lease or an operating lease:

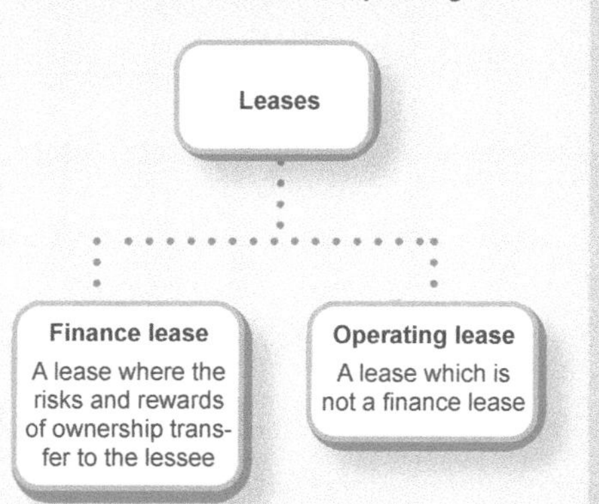

IFRS 16 gives the following indications that the risks and rewards of ownership have transferred to the lessee:

- Ownership is transferred at the end of the lease
- The lessee has the option to purchase the asset at the end of the lease term for less than fair value
- The lessee can continue to lease the asset at the end of the lease term for less than market rents
- The lease term is for the major part of the asset's life
- The present value of the minimum lease payments are substantially all of the fair value of the leased asset.

Lessor accounting treatment

Under a finance lease, the lessor must:

- derecognise the leased asset
- recognise a lease receivable at the present value of the minimum lease payments plus the estimated unguaranteed residual value of the asset
- recognise income on the lease receivable using the rate implicit in the lease.

Under an operating lease, the lessor must:

- continue to recognise and depreciate the leased asset
- recognise lease rental income in profit or loss on a straight line basis.

Sale and leaseback

The treatment of a sale and leaseback depends on whether the 'sale' represents the satisfaction of a performance obligation (as per IFRS 15 Revenue from Contracts with Customers).

	Transfer is not a sale	Transfer is a sale
Seller-lessee	Continue to recognise asset Recognise a financial liability equal to proceeds received.	Derecognise the asset. Recognise a right-of-use asset as the proportion of the previous carrying amount that relates to the rights retained. Recognise a lease liability. A profit or loss on disposal will arise.
Buyer-lessor	Do not recognise the asset Recognise a financial asset equal to transfer proceeds.	Account for the asset purchase. Account for the lease by applying lessor accounting requirements.

Exam focus

Exam Kit questions in this area:

- Leria
- Crypto
- Anouk
- Cherry
- Stem

chapter

9

Employee benefits

In this chapter

- Overview.
- Pensions.
- Measurement of defined benefit pension assets and liabilities.
- Short-term and other long-term benefits.
- Termination benefits.

Overview

Exam focus

- Pension schemes are accounted for in accordance with IAS 19 Employee Benefits.
- You must be prepared to deal with computational and discussion elements.

Definition

Types of pension scheme

Defined contribution

An entity pays fixed contributions and will have no legal or constructive obligation to pay further contributions if the fund does not hold sufficient assets to pay all employee benefits.

Defined benefit

A pension scheme that is not a defined contribution scheme.

Pensions

For a defined contribution scheme, contributions payable are recognised as an expense in profit or loss.

The accounting treatment of a defined benefit scheme is covered in more detail in the next section.

Measurement of defined benefit pension assets and liabilities

IAS 19 requires that:

- **plan assets** are measured at their fair value at the end of the reporting period
- **plan liabilities** are measured on an actuarial basis and are discounted to present value at the end of the reporting period.

The net liability (deficit) or net asset (surplus) is reported at each reporting date.

Note that where there is a net asset, the **asset ceiling test** applies. This restricts the value of the net asset reported to the extent that it is regarded as recoverable.

Defined benefit plan movement

The following proforma shows the movement on the defined benefit deficit (or a surplus) over a reporting period:

	$
Net deficit/(asset) brought forward (Obligation bfd – assets bfd)	X/(X)
Net interest component	X/(X)
Service cost component	X
Contributions into plan	(X)
Benefits paid	–
	X/(X)
Remeasurement component (bal. fig)	X/(X)
Net deficit/(asset) carried forward (Obligation cfd – assets cfd)	X/(X)

Definitions

- **Current service cost** is the '**increase in the present value of the defined benefit obligation resulting from employee service in the current period**' (IAS 19, para 8). This is part of the service cost component.
- **Past service cost** is the '**change in present value of the defined benefit obligation for employee service in prior periods resulting from a plan amendment or curtailment in the current period**' (IAS 19, para 8). This is part of the service cost component.
- A **curtailment** arises when there is a significant reduction in the number of employees covered by a plan. Any gain or loss on curtailment is part of the service cost component.

- A **settlement** arises when an entity enters into a transaction to terminate all or part of the benefits due to one or more employees under a plan. This is part of the service cost component.
- **Net interest component** is the change in measurement in both the plan obligation and plan assets due to the passage of time. It is calculated by applying the discount rate for the liability to the net liability (or asset) at the start of the reporting period. This is charged (or credited) to profit or loss.
- **The remeasurement component** arises due to differences between assumptions and estimates made when accounting for the defined benefit plan, and what has actually happened. The remeasurement component is taken to other comprehensive income.

Plan amendments, curtailments and settlements

If there is a plan amendment, settlement or curtailment (PASC) then the effect of this is calculated by comparing the net defined benefit deficit before and after the event.

The Board have amended IAS 19 to clarify that the reporting entity must determine:

- the current service cost for the remainder of the reporting period after the PASC using the actuarial assumptions used to remeasure the net defined benefit liability
- net interest for the remainder of the reporting period after the PASC using the remeasured defined benefit deficit and the discount rate used to remeasure the defined benefit deficit.

Recognising the amounts in the financial statements

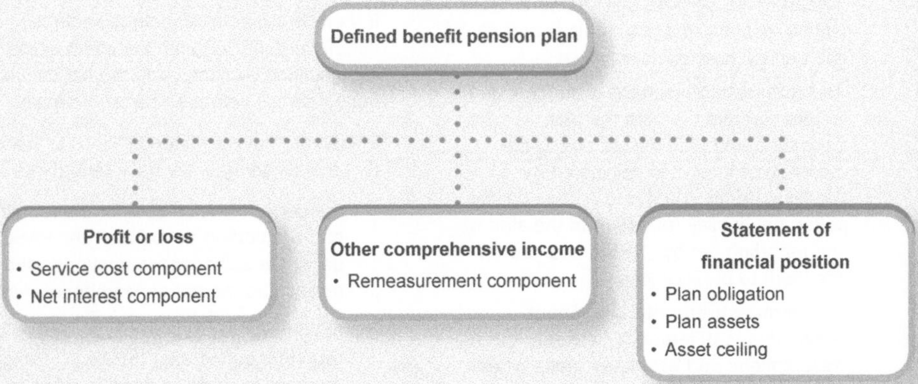

Defined benefit pension plan

Profit or loss

- Service cost component
- Net interest component

Other comprehensive income

- Remeasurement component

Statement of financial position

- Plan obligation
- Plan assets
- Asset ceiling

Short-term and other long-term benefits

Short-term benefits

This category includes items that will be settled within 12 months of the end of the reporting period when the employee provided the relevant service, such as wages and salaries. The costs are expensed as incurred in accordance with the accruals concept.

Other long-term benefits

This category includes items not expected to be settled within 12 months of the end of the reporting period when the employee provided the relevant service, such as deferred remuneration.

Other long-term benefits are accounted for in the same way as a defined benefit scheme, except that any remeasurement component is recorded in the statement of profit or loss.

Termination benefits

Definition

Termination benefits are benefits payable as a result of employment being terminated, either by the employer, or by the employee accepting voluntary redundancy.

Recognition

The reporting entity recognises a liability and expense at the earlier of the date when:

- the entity can no longer withdraw the termination benefits offer
- the entity recognises restructuring costs in accordance with IAS 37 Provisions, Contingent Liabilities and Contingent Assets.

Measurement

Termination benefits are measured on initial recognition.

Subsequent measurement depends on the nature of the benefit (i.e. whether it is short-term, a pension enhancement, or another type of long-term benefit).

Exam focus

Exam Kit questions in this area:

- Ecoma
- Digiwire
- Hudson
- Columbia
- Symbal

chapter

10

Share-based payment

In this chapter

- Overview.
- Accounting for share-based payments.
- Hybrid transactions.

Overview

IFRS 2 Share-based payment applies where an entity receives goods or services in exchange for shares, share options or cash based on a share price.

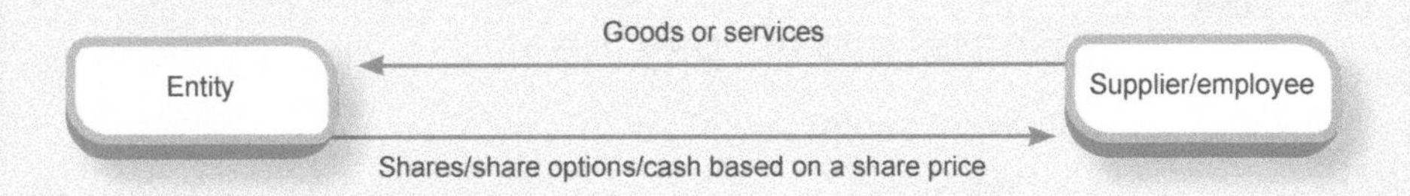

Recognising the transaction

The expense of a share-based payment scheme is accounted for over the vesting period based on the number of share-based payments expected to vest. If there are no vesting conditions, then the transaction is accounted for immediately.

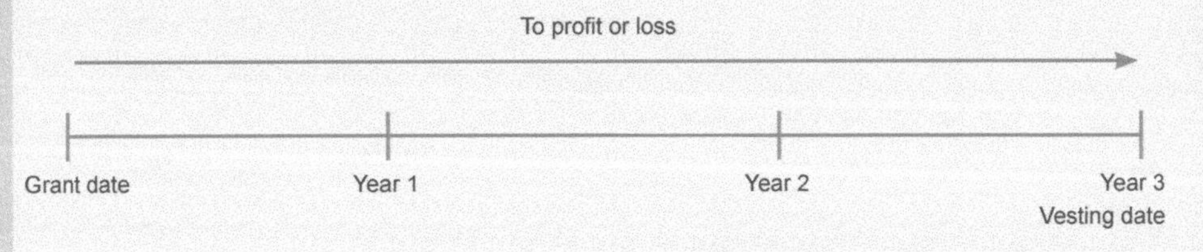

Definitions

Grant date: the date a share-based payment transaction is entered into.

Vesting date: the date on which the cash or equity instruments can be received by the other party to the agreement.

There are two types of share based payment transactions:

(1) **Equity-settled** share based payment transactions where a company receives goods or services in exchange for equity instruments (e.g. shares or share options).

(2) **Cash-settled** share based payment transactions, where a company receives goods and services in exchange for a cash amount paid based on its share price.

Accounting for share-based payments

Equity-settled share-based payments

The value of an equity-settled share-based payment transaction is determined as follows:

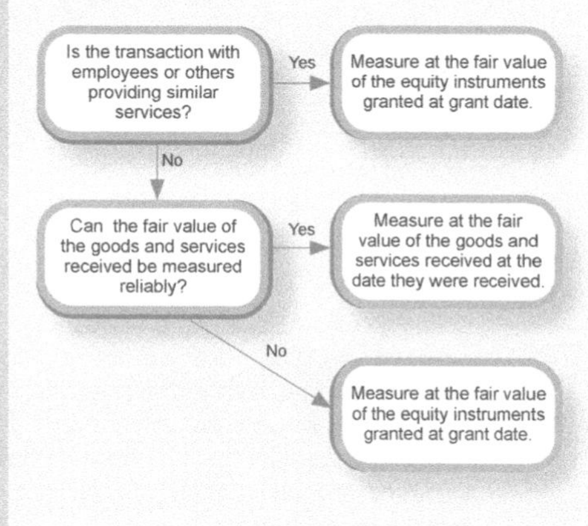

This should be recognised in profit or loss over the vesting period based on the number of shares or options that are expected to vest.

The accounting entry posted at each reporting date is:

Dr Profit or loss

Cr Equity

Modifications

If a modification to an equity-settled sharebased payment scheme occurs:

- the entity continues to recognise the grant date fair value of the equity instruments in profit or loss
- the entity also recognises an extra expense based on the difference between the fair value of the new arrangement and the fair value of the original arrangement (the incremental fair value) between the date of the change and the vesting date.

Cancellations

If an entity cancels or settles a share option scheme before the vesting date:

- The entity immediately recognises the amount that would otherwise have been recognised for services received over the vesting period (an acceleration of vesting)
- Any payment made to employees up to the fair value of the equity instruments at cancellation is accounted for as a deduction from equity.
- Any payment made to employees in excess of the fair value of the equity instruments at cancellation is accounted for as an expense in profit or loss.

Cash-settled share-based payments

Cash-settled schemes are often referred to as share-appreciation rights (SARs).

There are two key differences between the accounting treatment of SARs and an equity-settled share-based payment scheme:

- Until the settlement date, the expense is valued using the fair value of the SARs at the reporting date.
- The accounting entry required is:

  Dr Profit or loss

  Cr Liabilities

Hybrid transactions

Entity choice

If a share-based payment transaction gives the entity a choice over whether to settle in cash or by issuing equity instruments, IFRS 2 states that:

- The scheme is treated as a cash-settled share-based payment transaction if the entity has an obligation to settle in cash.
- If no obligation exists to settle in cash, then it is treated as an equity-settled share-based payment scheme.

Counterparty choice

If the share-based payment transaction gives the counterparty the choice of settling in cash or in equity instruments then the credit entry is split between equity and liabilities:

- If the transaction is with employees, the equity element is calculated as the fair value of the equity alternative at the grant date less the fair value of the cash alternative at the grant date.
- If the transaction is not with employees, the equity element is calculated as the fair value of the good or service received, less the fair value of the cash alternative at the date of the transaction.
- The liability element is calculated by taking the cash settlement option and applying the rules for cash-settled share-based payments.

The equity and liability components will be recognised over the vesting period.

Exam focus

Exam Kit questions in this area:

- Garden
- Margie

chapter

11

Provisions and events after the reporting period

In this chapter

- IAS 37 Provisions, contingent liabilities and contingent assets.
- IAS 10 Events after the reporting period.

IAS 37 Provisions, contingent liabilities and contingent assets

Definition

- A provision is '**a liability of uncertain timing or amount**' (IAS 37, para 10).
- A contingent liability is a possible obligation whose existence will be confirmed by uncertain future events outside of the entity's control.
- A contingent asset is a possible asset whose existence will be confirmed by uncertain future events outside of the entity's control.

Recognition

Recognise when:

- an entity has a present obligation (legal or constructive) as a result of a past event,
- it is probable that an outflow of economic benefits will be required, and
- a reliable estimate can be made.

Measurement

- The amount recognised should be the **best estimate** of the expenditure required to settle the obligation.
- Where the time value of money is material, the provision should be discounted to present value.

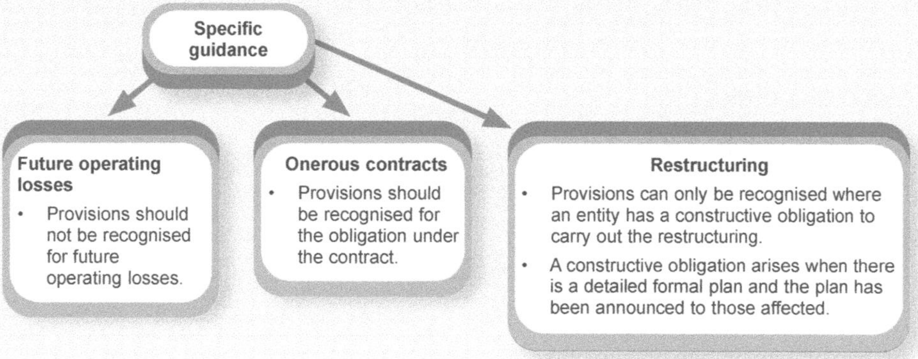

Specific guidance

Future operating losses

- Provisions should not be recognised for future operating losses.

Onerous contracts

- Provisions should be recognised for the obligation under the contract.

Restructuring

- Provisions can only be recognised where an entity has a constructive obligation to carry out the restructuring.
- A constructive obligation arises when there is a detailed formal plan and the plan has been announced to those affected.

Contingent liabilities should not be recognised. They should be disclosed unless the possibility of a transfer of economic benefits is remote.

Contingent assets should not be recognised. If the possibility of an inflow of economic benefits is probable they should be disclosed.

IAS 10 Events after the reporting period

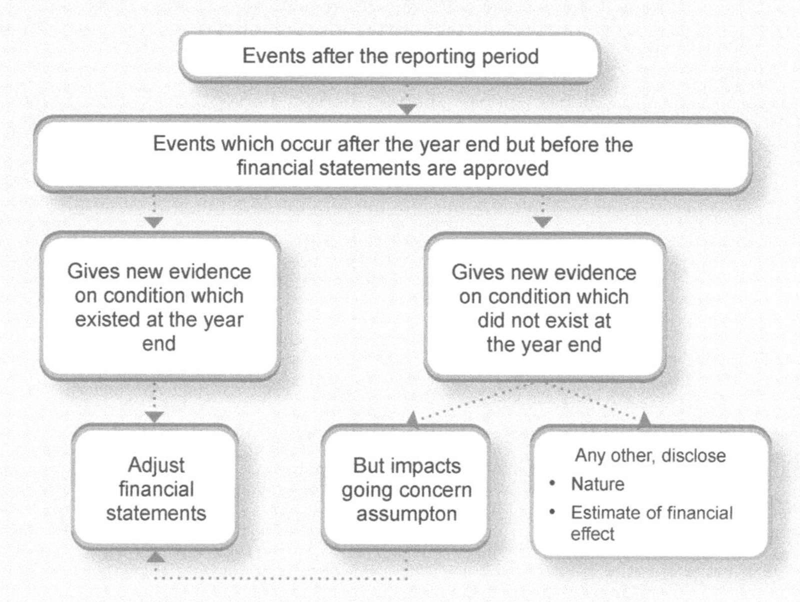

Exam focus

Exam Kit questions in this area:

- Mehran
- Colat

chapter

12

Financial instruments

In this chapter

- Definitions.
- Financial liabilities.
- Compound financial instruments.
- Financial assets.
- Financial asset impairments.
- Derecognition of financial instruments.
- Derivatives.
- Hedge accounting.
- Disclosure of financial instruments.

Definitions

A financial instrument is '**any contract that gives rise to a financial asset of one entity and a financial liability or equity instrument of another entity**' (IAS 32, para 11).

A **financial asset** is any asset that is:

- '**cash**
- **an equity instrument of another entity**
- **a contractual right to receive cash or another financial asset from another entity**
- **a contractual right to exchange financial instruments with another entity under conditions that are potentially favourable**' (IAS 32, para 11).

A **financial liability** is any liability that is a:

- '**contractual obligation to deliver cash or another financial asset to another entity**
- **contractual obligation to exchange financial instruments with another entity under conditions that are potentially unfavourable**
- **a contract that will or may be settled in the entity's own equity instruments, and is a non-derivative for which the entity is or may be obliged to deliver a variable number of the entity's own equity instruments**' (IAS 32, para 11).

An **equity instrument** is '**any contract that evidences a residual interest in the assets of an entity after deducting all of its liabilities**' (IAS 32, para 11).

Financial liabilities

Initial recognition

At initial recognition, financial liabilities are measured at fair value.

- If the financial liability will be held at fair value through profit or loss, transaction costs should be expensed to the statement of profit or loss.
- If the financial liability will not be held at fair value through profit or loss, transaction costs should be deducted from its carrying amount.

Subsequent treatment

The subsequent treatment of a financial liability is that they can be measured at either:

- amortised cost
- fair value through profit or loss.

Amortised cost

This category is used for most financial liabilities.

Interest income is calculated using the effective rate. This is charged to profit or loss and increases the carrying amount of the financial liability. Cash payments reduce the liability's carrying amount.

Fair value through profit or loss

This category is used for derivatives or liabilities held for trading.

The financial liability is revalued to fair value at the reporting date with the gain or loss in profit or loss.

A designation can be made to use this category in order to reduce an accounting mismatch. In this instance, the change in the fair value of the liability must be split:

- the change due to own credit risk is reported in OCI
- the remaining change is reported in profit or loss.

Compound financial instruments

A compound instrument is a financial instrument that has characteristics of both equity and liabilities. An example would be debt that can be redeemed either in cash or a fixed number of equity shares.

IAS 32 requires issuers of compound instruments to split them into:

- a financial liability (the liability to repay the debt holder in cash)
- an equity instrument (the option to convert into shares).

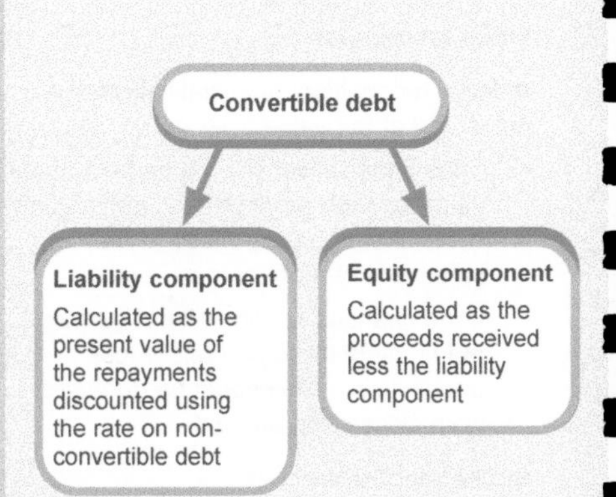

Financial assets

Initial recognition

At initial recognition, financial assets are measured at fair value.

- If the financial asset will be held at fair value through profit or loss, transaction costs should be expensed to the statement of profit or loss.
- If the financial asset will not be held at fair value through profit or loss, transaction costs should be added to its carrying amount.

Investments in equity

Investments in equity instruments (such as an investment in the ordinary shares of another entity) are normally measured at fair value through profit or loss.

It is possible to measure an equity instrument at fair value through other comprehensive income, provided that:

- the equity instrument is not held for trading, and
- an irrevocable choice for this designation is made upon initial recognition of the asset.

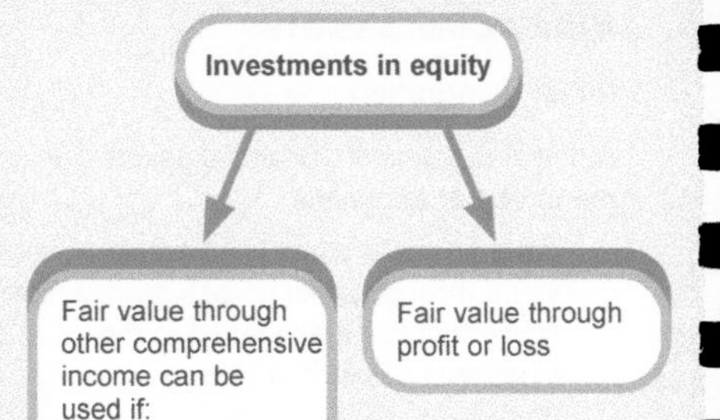

Investments in debt

Financial assets that are debt instruments can be measured in one of three ways:

1. An investment in a debt instrument is measured at **amortised cost** if:
   - The financial asset is held within a business model whose aim is to collect the contractual cash flows.
   - The contractual terms of the financial asset give rise to cash flows that are solely payments of principal and interest on the principal amount outstanding.
2. An investment in a debt instrument is measured at **fair value through other comprehensive income** if:
   - The financial asset is held within a business model whose objective is achieved by both collecting contractual cash flows and selling financial assets.
   - The contractual terms of the financial asset give rise to cash flows that are solely payments of principal and interest on the principal amount outstanding.
3. An investment in a debt instrument that is not measured at amortised cost or fair value through other comprehensive income will be measured at **fair value through profit or loss.**

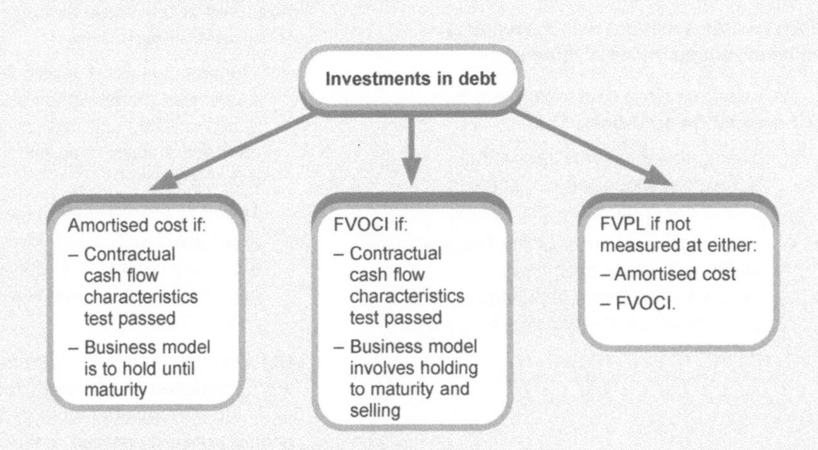
Investments in debt
Amortised cost if:
– Contractual cash flow characteristics test passed
– Business model is to hold until maturity
FVOCI if:
– Contractual cash flow characteristics test passed
– Business model involves holding to maturity and selling
FVPL if not measured at either:
– Amortised cost
– FVOCI.

Financial asset impairments

The impairment rules in IFRS 9 apply to debt instruments measured at amortised cost or at fair value through other comprehensive income.

For financial assets within the scope of the impairment rules, entities must calculate a loss allowance.

Increases and decreases in the loss allowance are charged to profit or loss.

This loss allowance must be equal to:

- **12 month expected credit losses** if credit risk has not increased significantly
- **Lifetime expected credit losses** if credit risk has increased significantly.

Definitions

Credit loss: the present value of the difference between the contractual cash flows due to an entity and the cash flows that it expects to receive.

Expected credit loss: the weighted average credit losses.

Lifetime expected credit losses: The expected credit losses that result from all possible default events.

12 month expected credit losses: The proportion of the lifetime expected credit losses that arise from default events within 12 months of the reporting date.

Derecognition of financial instruments

Key Point

A financial asset should be derecognised if one of the following has occurred:

- the contractual rights to the cash flows of the financial asset have expired.
- the financial asset has been sold and substantially all the **risks and rewards of ownership** have been transferred from the seller to the buyer.

A financial liability should be derecognised when the obligation specified in the contract is discharged, cancelled or has expired.

The accounting treatment of derecognition is as follows:

- The difference between the carrying amount of the asset or liability and the amount received or paid should be recognised in profit or loss for the period.
- For investments in equity instruments held at fair value through other comprehensive income, the cumulative gains and losses recognised in other comprehensive income are **not reclassified** to profit or loss on disposal.
- For investments in debt instruments held at fair value through other comprehensive income, the cumulative gains and losses recognised in other comprehensive income **are reclassified** to profit or loss on disposal.

Derivatives

Definitions

A derivative is a financial instrument with the following characteristics:

(a) Its value changes in response to an underlying variable.

(b) It requires little or no initial investment.

(c) It is settled at a future date.

Derivatives are measured at fair value through profit or loss.

Hedge accounting

Types of hedge accounting

A fair value hedge

'A hedge of the exposure to changes in fair value of a recognised asset or liability or an unrecognised firm commitment that is attributable to a particular risk and could affect profit or loss (or other comprehensive income for equity investments measured at fair value through other comprehensive income)' (IFRS 9, para 6.5.2).

A cash flow hedge

'A hedge of the exposure to variability in cash flows that is attributable to a particular risk associated with a recognised asset or liability or a highly probable forecast transaction and that could affect profit or loss' (IFRS 9, para 6.5.2).

Key Point

Derivatives introduce volatility into profit or loss. Hedge accounting is a method of managing this by designating one or more hedging instruments so that their change in fair value is offset, in whole or in part, by the change in fair value or cash flows of a hedged item.

Criteria

Under IFRS 9, hedge accounting rules can only be applied if the hedging relationship meets the following:

- The hedge consists of eligible hedging instruments and hedged items.
- At the inception of the hedge formal documentation identifies the hedged item and the hedging instrument.
- The hedging relationship is effective.
- If the hedged item is a forecast transaction, then the transaction must be highly probable.

A hedging relationship is effective if the following three criteria are met:

1. **'There is an economic relationship between the hedged item and the hedging instrument.**
2. **The effect of credit risk does not dominate the value changes that result from that economic relationship.**
3. **The hedge ratio of the hedging relationship is the same as that resulting from the quantity of the hedged item that the entity actually hedges and the quantity of the hedging instrument that the entity actually uses to hedge that quantity of hedged item**' (IFRS 9, para 6.4.1).

Accounting treatment of a fair value hedge

At the reporting date:

- the hedging instrument will be remeasured to fair value
- the carrying amount of the hedged item will be adjusted for the change in fair value since the inception of the hedge.

The gain (or loss) on the hedging instrument and the loss (or gain) on the hedged item will be recorded:

- in profit or loss in most cases, but
- in other comprehensive income if the hedged item is an investment in equity that is measured at fair value through other comprehensive income.

Accounting treatment of a cash flow hedge

For cash flow hedges, the hedging instrument will be remeasured to fair value at the reporting date.

- The gain or loss is recognised in other comprehensive income.
- However, if the gain or loss on the hedging instrument since the inception of the hedge is greater than the loss or gain on the hedged item then the **excess** gain or loss on the instrument must be recognised in profit or loss.

Discontinuing hedge accounting

An entity must cease hedge accounting if any of the following occur:

- The hedging instrument expires or is exercised, sold or terminated.
- The hedge no longer meets the hedging criteria.
- A forecast future transaction that qualified as a hedged item is no longer highly probable.

The discontinuance should be accounted for prospectively (entries posted to date are not reversed).

Disclosure of financial instruments

IFRS 7 Financial Instruments: Disclosures requires that entities disclose.

1. Information about the significance of financial instruments for an entity's financial position and performance.
2. Information about the nature and extent of risks arising from financial instruments.

Exam focus

Exam Kit questions in this area:

- Digiwire
- Crypto
- Aron
- Artwright
- Bismuth
- Colat

chapter

13

Tax

In this chapter

- Introduction to taxation.
- Deferred tax.
- Calculating deferred tax.
- Accounting for deferred tax.
- Specific scenarios.

Introduction to taxation

There are two elements to tax that an entity has to deal with:

Current tax – the amount payable to the tax authorities in relation to the trading activities of the current period.

Deferred tax – an accounting measure used to match the tax effects of transactions with their accounting treatment.

In summary, the tax expense for an entity is calculated as follows:

Tax expense = current tax +/– movement in deferred tax.

Deferred tax

According to the accruals concept, the tax effect of a transaction should be reported in the same accounting period as the transaction itself.

Deferred tax is recognised on temporary differences between the accounting and tax treatment of a transaction.

IAS 12 Income Taxes states that a **temporary difference** is the difference between the carrying amount of an asset or liability and its tax base.

Examples of temporary differences include (but are not restricted to):

- Tax deductions for the cost of non-current assets that have a different pattern to the write off of the asset in the financial statements.
- Assets are revalued upwards in the financial statements, but no adjustment is made for tax purposes.
- Development costs are capitalised and amortised to profit or loss in future periods, but were deducted for tax purposes as incurred.

Calculating deferred tax

The first step is to determine the temporary differences:

- If the carrying amount exceeds the tax base, the temporary difference is said to be a taxable temporary difference (a liability).
- If the tax base exceeds the carrying amount, the temporary difference is a deductible temporary difference (an asset).

The tax rate in force (or expected to be in force) when the asset is realised or the liability is settled is applied to the temporary difference to calculate the deferred tax balance.

This rate must be based on legislation enacted or substantively enacted by the reporting date.

Deferred tax assets and liabilities are **not** discounted to present value.

Accounting for deferred tax

The entry to profit or loss and other comprehensive income in respect of deferred tax is the difference between the net liability/ asset at the beginning of the year and the net liability/asset at the end of the year:

- If the item giving rise to the deferred tax is dealt with in profit or loss, the related deferred tax should also be presented in profit or loss.
- If the item giving rise to the deferred tax is dealt with in other comprehensive income, the related deferred tax should be recorded in other comprehensive income.

Specific scenarios

Share option schemes

The amount of tax relief granted is based on the intrinsic value of the options (the difference between the market price of the shares and the exercise price of the option) at the exercise date. This delayed tax relief gives rise to a deferred tax asset.

Unused tax losses

Where an entity has unused tax losses, IAS 12 allows a deferred tax asset to be recognised to the extent that it is probable that future taxable profits will be available against which the unused tax losses can be utilised.

Leases

If a lease transaction results in equal amounts of deductible and taxable temporary differences being created, then both a deferred tax asset and deferred tax liability should be recognised.

Business combinations

A business combination has deferred tax consequences:

- The identifiable net assets of the acquired subsidiary are consolidated at fair value but the tax base derives from the values in the subsidiary's individual financial statements. A temporary difference is created, giving rise to deferred tax in the consolidated financial statements.
- Provisions for unrealised profits reduce the carrying amount of inventory in the consolidated financial statements but the tax base is its cost in the individual financial statements. A temporary difference is created, giving rise to a deferred tax asset in the consolidated financial statements.

Goodwill itself does not give rise to deferred tax because IAS 12 specifically excludes it.

Exam focus

Exam Kit questions in this area:

- Hudson
- Holls
- Emcee
- Chuckle

chapter

14

Segment reporting

In this chapter

- IFRS 8 Operating segments.

IFRS 8 Operating segments

IFRS 8 Operating Segments requires a listed entity to disclose information about each of its operating segments.

Definition

An **operating segment** is a component of an entity:

- that engages in business activities
- whose operating results are regularly reviewed by the entity's chief operating decision maker
- that has discrete financial information available.

Aggregation

Two or more operating segments can be reported as a single operating segment provided that they have similar economic characteristics, and they are similar in terms of:

- the products or services they sell
- production processes
- types of customers
- distribution methods.

Reporting thresholds

An entity must separately report information about an operating segment that meets any of the following quantitative thresholds:

- **'its reported revenue, both sales to external customers and inter segment sales, is 10 per cent or more of the combined revenue of all operating segments.**

- **its reported profit or loss is 10 per cent or more of the greater, in absolute amount, of:**
  - **the combined reported profit of all operating segments that did not report a loss and**
  - **the combined reported loss of all operating segments that reported a loss.**
- **its assets are 10 per cent or more of the combined assets of all operating segments**' (IFRS 8, para 13).

At least 75% of the entity's external revenue should be included in reportable segments. This means that other segments might need to be identified as reportable segments until this 75% threshold is reached.

Disclosures

IFRS 8 requires detailed disclosures, including:

- factors used to identify the entity's reportable segments
- the types of products and services sold by each reportable segment.

For each reportable segment an entity should report:

- a measure of profit or loss
- a measure of total assets
- a measure of total liabilities (if this amount is used in decision making).

Exam Focus

Exam Kit questions in this area:

- Garden
- Klancet

chapter

15

Related parties

In this chapter

- Related parties.
- Importance of related party disclosures.
- Related party disclosures.

Related parties

Exam Focus

- Related party transactions can affect the performance and position of an entity.
- In the exam you may have to determine related party transactions and the ethical implications of these.

Definition

IAS 24 Related Party Disclosures says that a person, or member of their close family, is related to the reporting entity if they:

- have control or joint control over the entity
- have significant influence over the reporting entity
- are a member of key management personnel of the entity or its parent.

Two entities are related if:

- they are parents and subsidiaries within the same group
- one entity is an associate or joint venture of the other
- a person (or a member of their close family) who is a related party of one of the entities has control over the other
- a person who has control over one of the entities also has significant influence over the other entity or is a member of its (or its parent's) key management personnel.

Summary

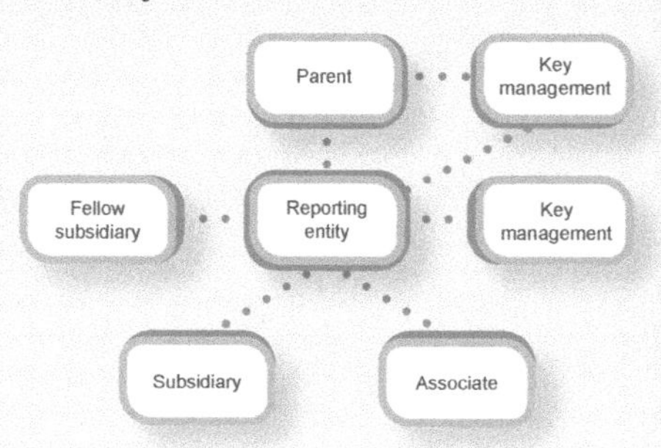

Definition

A **related party transaction** is the '**transfer of resources, services or obligations between related parties regardless of whether a price is charged**' (IAS 24, para 6).

Importance of related party disclosures

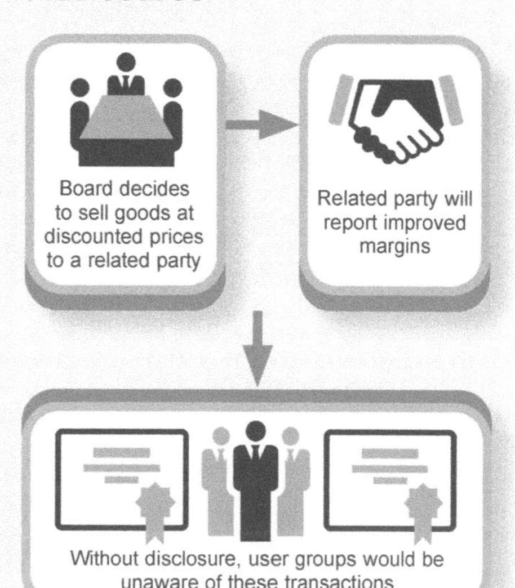

Related party disclosures

- Relationships between parents and subsidiaries.
- The name of the parent and the ultimate controlling party (if different).
- Key management personnel compensation.
- For related party transactions that have occurred disclosures should include:

  (a) the amount of the transactions

  (b) the amount of outstanding balances and their terms

  (c) allowances for doubtful debts relating to the outstanding balances

  (d) the expense recognised in the period in respect of irrecoverable or doubtful debts.

Exam Focus

Exam Kit questions in this area:

- Stent
- Garden

chapter

16

Adoption of International Financial Reporting Standards

In this chapter

- IFRS 1 First time adoption of International Financial Reporting Standards.
- Practical factors.

IFRS 1 First time adoption of International Financial Reporting Standards

This standard sets out the procedures to be followed in adopting IFRS Standards for the first time.

Definition

IFRS 1 defines the **date of transition** as the beginning of the earliest period for which an entity presents full comparative information in its first financial statements prepared under IFRS Standards.

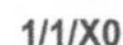

1/1/X0
The date of transition to IFRS (The first day of the comparative period)

31/12/X0
Comparative figures for first set of published IFRS financial statements

31/12/X1
First set of published IFRS financial statements

Adoption of IFRS Standards

IFRS 1 states that the opening IFRS statement of financial position at the date of transition must:

- recognise all assets and liabilities required by IFRS Standards
- not recognise assets and liabilities not permitted by IFRS Standards
- reclassify all assets, liabilities and equity components in accordance with IFRS Standards
- measure all assets and liabilities in accordance with IFRS Standards.

Gains and losses arising on transition to IFRS Standards are recorded in retained earnings.

Practical factors

Before adopting a new set of accounting standards, an entity should consider the following:

- Bonuses and performance related pay – impact of profit changes?
- IT systems – will they require updating or replacing?
- Covenants on loans – will they be breached?
- Earnings per share – will it reduce?
- Perception – will analysts view the move positively?
- Staff knowledge – is it sufficient?

Exam focus

Exam Kit questions in this area:

- Whitebirk

chapter

17

Small and medium entities

In this chapter

- Small and medium-sized entities.
- The IFRS for SMEs Standard.

Small and medium sized entities

Definition

A small and medium sized entity (SME) is an entity that:

(1) does not have public accountability and

(2) publishes general purpose financial statements for external users.

The IFRS for SMEs Standard

Background

The IFRS for SMEs Standard was issued for use by entities that have no public accountability.

This standard reduces the burden of producing information that is not likely to be of interest to the stakeholders of a small or medium company.

Exam focus

The exam may ask you to discuss the differences between full IFRS Standards and the IFRS for SMEs Standard.

Omissions from the SMEs Standard

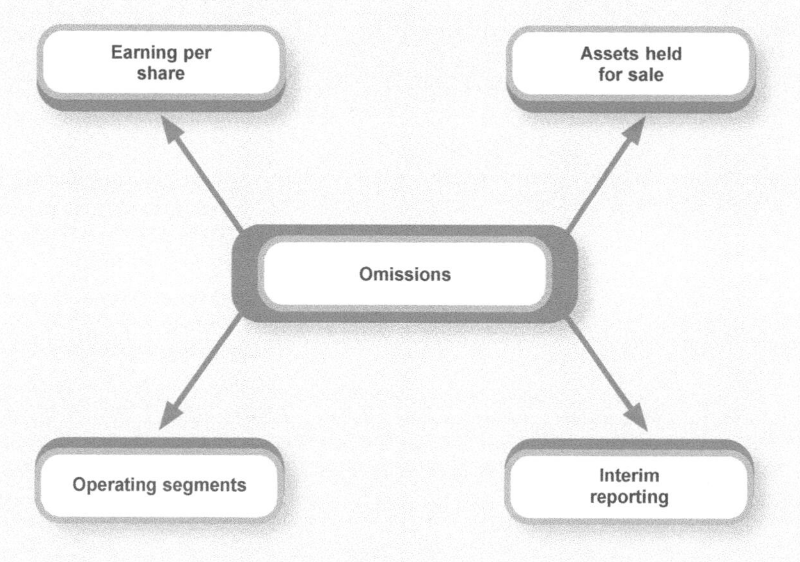

Disallowed treatments in the SMEs Standard

- The non-controlling interest at the acquisition date **cannot** be measured at fair value.
- The revaluation model **cannot** be used for intangible assets.
- The cost model for investment property is **only** used if the fair value cannot be determined reliably.

Simplifications in the SMEs Standard

- Borrowing costs are always expensed to profit or loss.
- Depreciation and amortisation methods do not need to be reviewed annually.
- Expenditure on research and development is always expensed to profit or loss.
- Goodwill is amortised over its useful life. If the useful life cannot be reliably established then an estimate of ten years or less should be used.
- Cumulative exchange differences are not recycled to profit or loss on the disposal of an overseas subsidiary.
- Simplified techniques are permitted when measuring a defined benefit obligation.

Exam focus

Exam Kit questions in this area:

- Handfood
- Whitebirk

chapter

18

Group accounting – basic groups

In this chapter

- Overview.
- IFRS 10 Consolidated financial statements.
- Business combinations.
- The acquisition method.
- Goodwill impairment.
- Basic workings.
- Associates.
- Joint arrangements.
- IFRS 12 Disclosure of interests in other entities.
- IAS 27 Separate financial statements.

Overview

Exam focus

- Question one will always test group accounting.
- The SBR exam is likely to require discussion of issues in consolidated financial statement and/or the production of extracts.

IFRS 10 Consolidated financial statements

Definition

A **parent** is an entity that controls another entity.

A **subsidiary** is an entity that is controlled by a parent entity.

IFRS 10 says that an investor has control when it has:

- power over the investee
- exposure, or rights to, variable returns from involvement in the investee
- the ability to use power over the investee to affect the investor's returns.

An entity that is a parent is required to produce consolidated financial statements.

Business combinations

IFRS 3 Business Combinations states that the acquisition method is used to account for business combinations.

Definition

A business combination is where an acquirer obtains control of a business.

Concentration test

An optional concentration test can be used to assess whether an acquired set of assets is **not** a business.

The acquired assets are not a business if substantially all of the fair value of the total assets acquired is concentrated in a single identifiable asset or group of similar identifiable assets.

Elements of a business

If the concentration test is not met, or if the test is not applied, a detailed assessment is required to assess if a business has been acquired.

To meet the definition of a business, inputs and substantive processes must have been acquired that can contribute to the creation of outputs.

Definition

Inputs are economic resources that can create outputs once processes are applied.

Processes are systems, standards or rules that can create outputs when applied to inputs.

Outputs include goods, services and income.

The acquisition method

The acquisition method has four requirements.

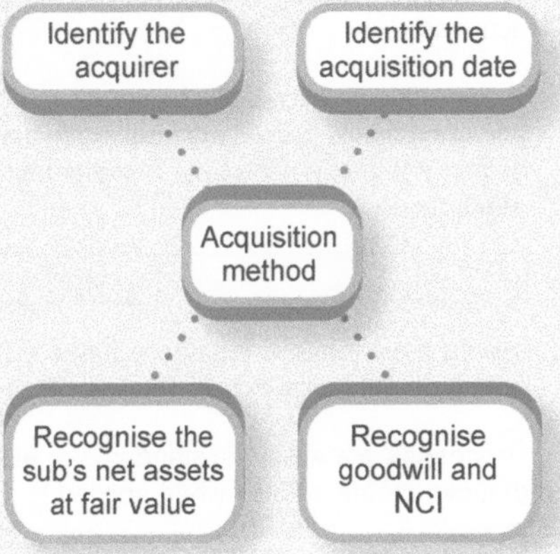

Identify the acquirer

The acquirer is the entity that has assumed control over another entity.

The acquirer is **normally** the company that has **transferred cash**, other assets or **shares** in the business combination.

Other factors to consider include:

- which entity's former management dominates the combined entity?
- which entity's former owners have the greatest number of votes in the combined entity?
- which entity was bigger?

Identify the acquisition date

This is the date on which the parent obtained control over the subsidiary.

Recognise the net assets

The acquirer must measure the identifiable assets acquired and the liabilities assumed at their **fair values** at the acquisition date.

Recognise goodwill and the NCI

When calculating goodwill, **purchase consideration** is measured at **fair value**.

Professional fees are **expensed** to profit or loss.

The non-controlling interest at acquisition can either be measured:

- at **fair value** – this calculates full goodwill (P's goodwill + NCI's goodwill)
- its **proportionate share** of the fair value of the subsidiary's identifiable net assets – this calculates P's goodwill only.

Goodwill impairment

Goodwill is tested annually for impairment.

Goodwill does not generate independent cash flows and so is tested for impairment as part of a **cash-generating unit**. For exam purposes, this is normally a subsidiary.

Definition

A cash-generating unit is the smallest group of assets that generate cash inflows that are independent from other cash inflows in the business.

Key Point

Whether the NCI at acquisition was measured at fair value or proportionately has a significant impact on the impairment review:

- **Fair value method** – the group has recognised full goodwill so this can be added together with the other net assets of the subsidiary and compared with the recoverable amount.
- **Proportionate method** – only the group's share of goodwill has been recognised, so goodwill must be grossed up to include the NCI's share prior to performing the impairment review.

Basic workings

The SBR exam is unlikely to ask you to prepare full consolidated financial statements. However, the following workings are still useful when producing extracts.

Consolidated statement of financial position	**$000**
Goodwill (W3)	X
Assets (P + S)	X
Total assets	X
Share capital (P's only)	X
Other components of equity (W5)	X
Retained earnings (W5)	X
NCI (W4)	X
Total equity	X
Liabilities (P + S)	X
Total equity and liabilities	X

Set out your workings as follows:

W1 Group structure

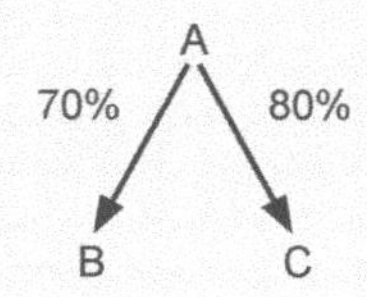

W2 Net assets of each subsidiary

	At acquisition date	At reporting date
	$000	$000
Equity share capital	X	X
Other components of equity	X	X
Retained earnings	X	X
Fair value adjustments	X /(X)	X /(X)
Post-acq'n accounting adjustments e.g. PURP on sales made by S		X /(X)
	X	X
	To W3	

W3 Goodwill

	$000
FV of consideration	X
NCI at acquisition	X
	X
FV of net assets at acquisition (W2)	(X)
Goodwill at acquisition	X
Impairment to date	(X)
Goodwill at reporting date	X

W4 Non-controlling interest

	$000
NCI at acquisition (W3)	X
NCI% x post-acquisition reserves (W2)	X
Less: NCI% of goodwill impairment (W3) (FV method only)	(X)
	X

W5 Group reserves

Retained earnings

	$000
Parent company (100%)	X
Subsidiary: Group share of post acquisition retained earnings (W2)	X
Less goodwill impairment (W3)*	(X)
PURP if P is seller	(X)
	——
	X
	——

*P% only if FV method used

Other components of equity

	$000
Parent company	X
Subsidiary: Group share of post-acquisition other components of equity (W2)	X
	——
	X
	——

Consolidated statement of profit or loss and other comprehensive income

Step 1: Group structure

Step 2: Set up the pro-forma

	$000
Revenue (P + S)	X
Cost of sales (P + S)	(X)
Gross profit	X
Operating costs (P + S)	(X)
Operating profit	X
Finance costs (P + S)	(X)
Profit before tax	X
Tax (P + S)	(X)
Profit for the period	Y
Other comprehensive income (P + S)	X
Total comprehensive income (TCI)	Z
Profit attributable to:	
Equity holders of group (bal.)	X
Non-controlling interest (step 4)	X
	Y
TCI attributable to:	
Equity holders of group (bal.)	X
Non-controlling interest (step 4)	X
	Z

Step 3: Complete the pro-forma

Add together the parent and subisidiary's income and expenses and items of other comprehensive income on a line-by-line basis.

- If the subsidiary has been acquired mid-year, pro-rate the results of the subsidiary so that only post-acquisition income, expenses and other comprehensive income are consolidated.
- Eliminate intra-group income and expenses, unrealised profits on intra-group transactions, as well as any dividends received from the subsidiary.

Step 4: Calculate the profit/TCI attributable to the non-controlling interest

	Profit	TCI
	$000	$000
Profit/TCI of the subsidiary for the year (pro-rated for mid-year acquisition)	X	X
PURP (if S is the seller)	(X)	(X)
Excess depreciation/amortisation	(X)	(X)
Goodwill impairment (under FV model only)	(X)	(X)
	———	———
× NCI %	X	X
	———	———
Profit/TCI attributable to the NCI	X	X

Associates

Definition

- IAS 28 Accounting for Associates and Joint Ventures defines an associate as '**an entity over which the investor has significant influence**' (IAS 28, para 3).
- Significant influence is the power to participate in the financial and operating policy decisions of an entity.
- A holding of between 20% and 50% of the voting power is presumed to give significant influence.

Accounting for associates

Associates are accounted for using the equity method.

Statement of financial position

	$000
Cost	X
Add: share of increase in net assets	X
Less: impairment losses	(X)
Investment in Associate	X

Profit or loss

Include the group's share of the associate's **profit after tax less any impairment losses**.

Joint arrangements

Definition

Joint arrangements are defined in IFRS 11 Joint arrangements as arrangements where '**two or more parties have joint control**' (IFRS 11, para 4). This exists when the relevant activities require unanimous consent of the parties that share control.

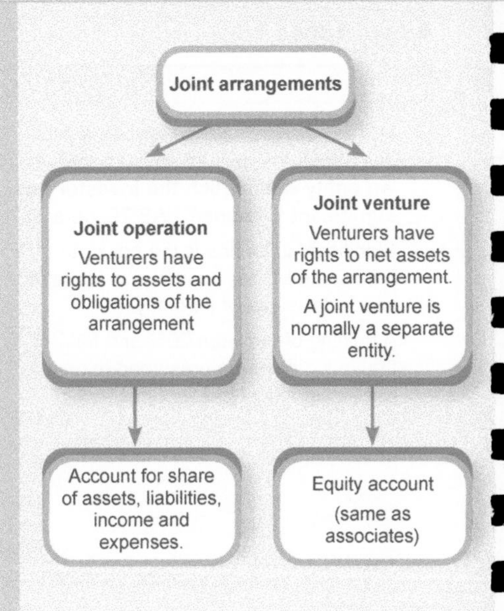

IFRS 12 Disclosure of interests in other entities

IFRS 12 outlines the disclosures required when one entity has an investment in another.

IAS 27 Separate financial statements

IAS 27 applies when an entity has interests in subsidiaries, joint ventures or associates and it prepares separate non-consolidated financial statements.

In separate financial statements, investments in subsidiaries, joint ventures or associates can be accounted for in one of the following ways:

- cost
- in accordance with IFRS 9 Financial Instruments, or
- using the equity method.

Exam focus

Exam Kit questions in this area:

- Luploid
- Banana
- Trailer
- Columbia
- Stem

chapter

19

Change in a group structure

In this chapter

- Overview.
- Step acquisition.
- Disposal of subsidiaries where control is lost.
- Presentation of disposal.
- Control to control scenarios.

Overview

This chapter concerns the impact of different types of share purchases and share sales on the consolidated financial statements.

Step acquisition

A step acquisition occurs when the parent company acquires control over the subsidiary in stages. Acquisition accounting is only applied at the date when control is achieved.

At the date control is achieved:

(1) re-measure the previously held equity interest to fair value

(2) recognise any resulting gain or loss in profit or loss for the year (or in OCI if the shares were FVOCI)

(3) calculate goodwill and the non-controlling interest.

For the purposes of the goodwill calculation, use the following proforma:

	$000
Fair value of previously held interest	X
Fair value of consideration for additional interest	X
NCI at acquisition	X
	X
Less: FV of net assets at acquisition	(X)
Goodwill at acquisition	X

Disposal of subsidiaries where control is lost

If the sale of shares causes control over a subsidiary to be lost, then the treatment in the consolidated financial statements is as follows:

- Consolidate the income and expenses of the subsidiary up until the disposal date.
- On disposal of the subsidiary, derecognise its assets, liabilities, goodwill and non-controlling interest and calculate a profit or loss on disposal.
- Recognise any remaining investment in the shares of the former subsidiary at fair value and subsequently account for this under the relevant accounting standard.
  - A holding of 20-50% of the shares would probably mean that the remaining investment is an associate, which should be accounted for using the equity method.
  - A holding of less than 20% of the shares would probably mean that the remaining investment should be accounted for under IFRS 9 Financial Instruments.

The profit or loss on disposal is calculated as follows:

	$000	$000
Disposal proceeds		X
Fair value of retained interest		X
		——
		X
Less interest in subsidiary disposed of:		
Net assets of subsidiary at disposal date	X	
Goodwill at disposal date	X	
Less: Carrying amount of NCI at disposal date	(X)	
	——	
		(X)
		——
Profit/(loss) to the group		X/(X)
		——

Presentation of disposal

If a subsidiary is acquired exclusively with a view to subsequent disposal and it meets the held for sale criteria in IFRS 5:

– it is presented in the financial statements as a disposal group classified as held for sale. This is achieved by amalgamating all its assets into one line item and all its liabilities into another

– it is measured, both on acquisition and at subsequent reporting dates, at fair value less costs to sell.

Control to control scenarios

Share purchases

Some share purchases simply increase the parent's holding in a subsidiary.

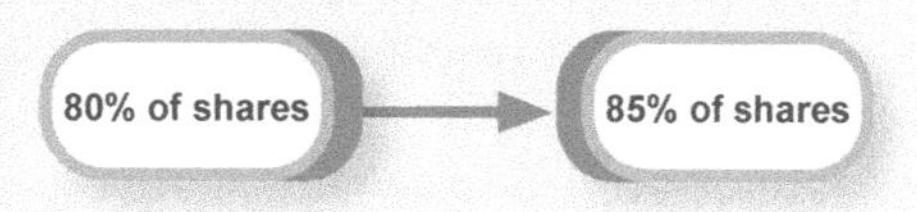

In such instances:

- Goodwill is **not** recalculated
- A profit or loss **does not** arise in the consolidated financial statements.

The entry in the consolidated financial statements is:

Dr Non-controlling interest	X
Cr Cash	X
Dr/Cr Other components of equity	X (bal. fig.)

The decrease in NCI is calculated as the proportionate reduction in its carrying amount at the date of the group's additional purchase of shares.

Share sales

Some share sales simply reduce the parent's holding in a subsidiary but do not lead to a loss of control.

In such instances:

- Goodwill is **not** recalculated
- A profit or loss **does not** arise in the consolidated financial statements.

The entry in the consolidated financial statements is:

Dr Cash	X
Cr Non-controlling interest	X
Dr/Cr Other components of equity	X (bal. fig.)

The increase in the NCI will be the share of the net assets (always) and goodwill (fair value method only) of the subsidiary at the date of disposal which the parent has effectively sold to the NCI.

Exam focus

Exam Kit questions in this area:

- Zippy
- Ashanti
- Chuckle
- Sitka

chapter

20

Group accounting – foreign currency

In this chapter

- Foreign subsidiaries.
- Proformas.
- Other foreign operations.

Foreign subsidiaries

If a company has foreign subsidiaries whose functional currency is their local currency, their financial statements must be translated into the parent's presentation currency.

- All **assets and liabilities** are translated into the group's presentation currency using the **closing rate** of exchange.
- **Goodwill** is treated as an asset of the subsidiary. It is calculated using the functional currency of the subsidiary. It is then translated using the closing rate for inclusion in the group accounts.
- **Income and expenses** must be translated at the average rate for the period.
- **Exchange differences** arising on consolidation are recognised in other comprehensive income. On disposal of the subsidiary, they are recycled to the statement of profit or loss.
- Exchange differences arise from:
  - the retranslation of the opening net assets using the closing rate
  - retranslation of the the profit for the year from the average rate (used in the statement of profit or loss) to the closing rate (for inclusion in the statement of financial position)
  - the retranslation of goodwill at each reporting date using the closing rate.

Proformas

Opening net assets and profit

The exchange gains or losses arising on the translation of opening net assets and profit for the year are generally calculated together.

The proforma for calculating the current year exchange gain or loss on the translation of the opening net assets and profit is as follows:

	DN	Exchange Rate	$
Opening net assets	X	Opening rate	X
Profit/(loss) for the year	X/(X)	Average rate	X/(X)
Exchange gain/(loss)	–	**Bal fig.**	X/(X)
Closing net assets	X	Closing rate	X

Goodwill translation

The proforma for calculating the current year exchange gain or loss on the retranslation of goodwill is as follows:

	DN	Exchange Rate	$
Opening goodwill	X	Opening rate	X
Impairment loss in year	(X)	Average rate	(X)
Exchange gain/(loss)	–	**Bal fig.**	X/(X)
Closing goodwill	X	Closing rate	X

Other foreign operations

The rules covered in this chapter also apply to the translation of overseas associates and joint arrangements.

Remember that:

- **Income, expenses and other comprehensive income** are translated at the exchange rate in place at the date of each transaction. The average rate for the year may be used as an approximation.
- **Assets and liabilities** are translated at the closing rate of exchange.
- **Exchange gains and losses** are recognised in other comprehensive income.

Exam focus

Exam Kit questions in this area:

- Hummings
- Carbise
- Bubble
- Agency Group

chapter

21

Group statement of cash flows

In this chapter

- Overview.
- Format of the statement of cash flows.
- Cash generated from operations.
- Acquisitions and disposals.
- Dividends from associates.
- Dividends paid to non-controlling interests.

Overview

Key Point

- A statement of cash flows enables users of the financial statements to assess the **liquidity**, **solvency** and **financial adaptability** of a business.

Definition

- **Cash consists of** cash in hand and deposits repayable upon demand less overdrafts. This includes cash held in a foreign currency.
- **Cash equivalents** are '**short term, highly liquid investments that are readily convertible to known amounts of cash and are subject to an insignificant risk of changes in value**' (IAS 7, para 6).

Format of the statement of cash flows

IAS 7 Statement of Cash Flows requires that the statement is split into three sections – operating, investing and financing.

In the SBR exam you may be asked to produce extracts from a consolidated statement of cash flow.

DEF Group statement of cash flows for the year ended 31 December 20X6

	$000	$000
Cash flows from operating activities		
Profit before tax	X	
Adjustments for:		
Depreciation	X	
Impairment	X	
Profit on sale of non-current assets	(X)	
Share of associate profits	(X)	
Investment income	(X)	
Finance costs	X	
Increase in inventories	(X)	
Increase in receivables	(X)	
Increase in payables	X	
Cash generated from operations		X
Interest paid	(X)	
Income tax paid	(X)	
Net cash inflow from operating activities		X
Cash flows from investing activities		
Dividends received from associate	X	
Interest received	X	
Purchase of property, plant and equipment	(X)	
Proceeds from sale of property	X	
Acquisition of subsidiary, net of cash acquired	(X)	
Net cash used in investing activities		(X)

Cash flows from financing activities		
Issue of ordinary share capital	X	
Repayment of loan	(X)	
Dividends paid to NCI	(X)	
Dividends paid to parent shareholders	(X)	
Net cash used in financing activities		(X)
Net increase in cash and cash equivalents		X
Cash and cash equivalents brought forward		X
Cash and cash equivalents carried forward		X

Cash generated from operations

IAS 7 allows 'cash generated from operations' to be presented in one of two ways:

- **The indirect method** – this starts with profit before tax and adjusts it to remove the effect of non-cash transactions and transactions that relate to investing or financing activities (as per the pro-forma in the previous section)
- **The direct method** – this shows operating cash receipts and payments, such as cash receipts from customers, cash payments to suppliers, and cash payments to employees.

IAS 7 encourages the use of the direct method.

Acquisitions and disposals

The figure shown in the statement of cash flows is the net figure of two items.

- The cash spent on the purchase or received on the sale of the subsidiary.
- The cash balances (or overdraft). acquired or disposed of with a subsidiary.

The impact of subsidiary acquisitions and disposals will need to be factored into your workings throughout.

Dividends from associates

To find the dividend reconcile the opening and closing balance of the investment in the associate.

	$000
Associate b/fwd	X
Share of profit and OCI	X
Cash dividend received (**bal fig**)	(X)
Purchase of associates	X
Disposal of associates	(X)
Associate c/fwd	X

Dividends paid to non-controlling interests

Reconcile the opening to closing balance and the cash dividend paid is the balancing figure.

	$000
NCI b/fwd	X
Add: NCI on sub acquisition	X
Add: NCI share of profit and OCI	X
Less: NCI on sub disposal	(X)
Cash dividend paid (bal. fig)	(X)
NCI c/fwd	X

Exam focus

Exam Kit questions in this area:

- Sugar
- Moyes
- Jocatt

chapter

22

Analysis and Interpretation

In this chapter

- Purpose of financial reporting.
- Financial performance measures.
- Earnings per share.
- Additional performance measures.
- Non-financial information.
- Sustainability.
- Integrated reporting.

Exam Focus

Analysis and interpretation of information will always feature in Section B of the SBR exam.

Two professional marks will be available in this question.

Purpose of financial reporting

The purpose of financial reporting is to provide user groups with information that will help them to make decisions about providing resources to an entity.

Key user groups include:

- investors
- lenders
- other creditors, such as suppliers.

According to the Conceptual Framework, these users need information to assess:

- the entity's future cash flows
- management's stewardship of assets.

Financial performance measures

Calculating ratios helps users to understand an entity's financial performance and position and so can help users make investment decisions.

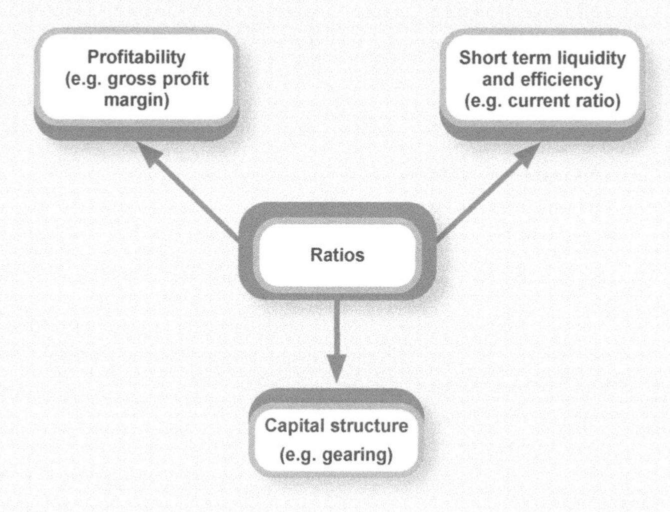

Earnings per share

Key Point

Earnings per share (EPS) is a ratio used to assess financial performance. In accordance with IAS 33 Earnings per Share, listed companies must disclose basic and diluted EPS.

Basic EPS

$$\frac{\text{Earnings attributable to ordinary shareholders}}{\text{Weighted average no.of ordinary shares}}$$

Diluted EPS

At the year-end, an entity may have a commitment to issue more ordinary shares. Such commitments include:

- convertible loans
- share options.

Diluted EPS is an estimate of the impact of these future share issues on an entity's EPS.

Exam Focus

The SBR exam is more likely to focus on the impact of errors on EPS rather than on the calculation of EPS.

Additional performance measures

Definition

Additional performance measures (APMs) are measures of performance not defined within IFRS Standards.

Types

Common APMs disclosed by entities include:

- **EBITDA** – earnings before interest, tax, depreciation and amortisation
- **Free cash flow** – cash flows from operating activities less capital expenditure.

Benefits

Benefits of disclosing APMs include:

- helping users to evaluate an entity through the eyes of management
- stripping out transactions that are not relevant to current or future year operating performance.

Drawbacks

APM disclosures have been criticised for:

- presenting an over-optimistic picture of the entity's performance
- giving undue prominence to figures that are not calculated in accordance with IFRS Standards.

Non-financial information

Criticisms of financial reporting

Financial performance measures:

- provide limited information about future performance
- do not provide information about key issues that impact long-term success, such as customer satisfaction
- can be manipulated through accounting estimates or policy choices.

Non-financial reporting measures

These are related to entity performance but are not expressed in monetary units. Examples include

- Employee turnover
- Customer satisfaction
- Delivery times

Sustainability

Goals

Sustainable Development Goals (SDGs) comprise 17 goals agreed by UN member states that include no poverty, zero hunger, reduced inequalities, and responsible production and consumption. They are only achievable through the cooperation of industry.

Companies should set sustainable development goals because:

- It is ethical
- Government funding will increasingly focus on sustainable businesses
- It reduces reputational and regulatory risk
- Sustainable products and services are a growth area
- Short-term, profit-based models are now less relevant for many investors.

Many investors are interested in companies that contribute to SDGs. Some will not invest in companies with low levels of pay or high levels of gender inequality.

Reporting Standards

There are many reporting initiatives that can be used to communicate progress towards SDGs:

- The United Nations Global Compact (UNGC)
- The Global Reporting Initiative (GRI)
- The International Integrated Reporting Framework.

Integrated reporting

Definition

An integrated report tells its users how the reporting entity creates value in the short, medium and long-term.

Value

Value is conceptualised in terms of capitals. The integrated reporting framework identifies six capitals:

- Financial
- Manufactured
- Intellectual
- Human
- Social and relationship
- Natural

An integrated report should detail the impact that the reporting entity's business model has on the full range of capitals.

Content of an integrated report

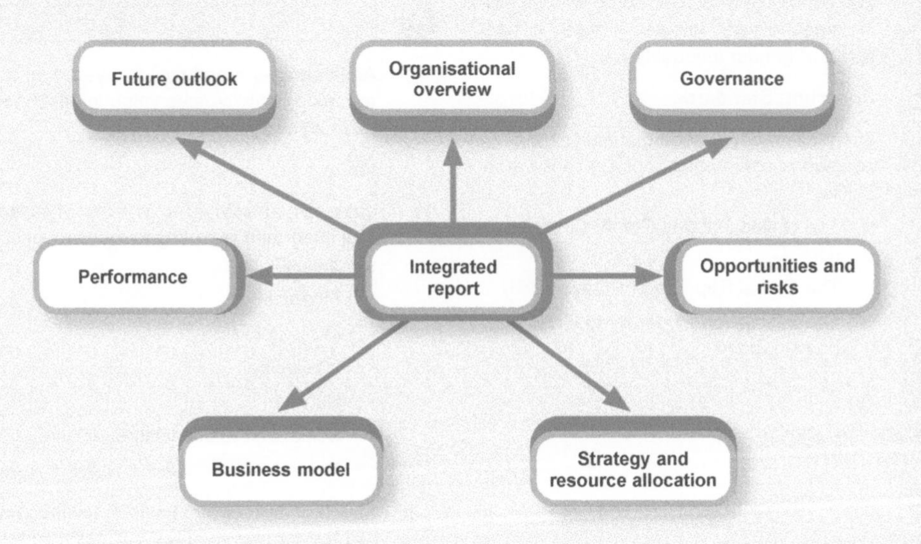

Exam Focus

Exam Kit questions in this area:

- Ecoma
- Guidance
- Crypto
- Toobasco
- Stem

chapter

23

Current issues

In this chapter

- What is a current issue?
- Contemporary business environment.
- Materiality.
- Management commentary.
- Developments in sustainability reporting.

Exam Focus

Current issues are central to the SBR syllabus. They are likely to be tested in every exam.

What is a current issue?

The SBR syllabus and examinable documents identify the following current issues:

- contemporary business environment
- materiality
- management commentary
- developments in sustainability reporting

Contemporary business environment

This section covers three contemporary issues: cryptocurrency, initial coin offerings, and natural disasters.

Cryptocurrency

Definition

Cryptocurrencies are virtual currencies that provide the holder with various rights. They are not issued by a central authority and so exist outside of governmental control.

The accounting treatment of cryptocurrency is unclear. Cryptocurrency is not:

- **cash** – not readily exchangeable for goods or services
- **a cash equivalent** – risk of value change too significant.
- **another type of financial instrument** – no contractual right to receive cash.

Cryptocurrency potentially falls within the scope of IAS 38 Intangible Assets. However this standard requires income or expense arising from fair value remeasurement to be presented in other comprehensive income rather than in profit or loss.

It may be that entities need to apply the Conceptual Framework (see Chapter 1) to develop an appropriate policy.

Initial coin offerings

Definition

Initial coin offerings (ICO) are a method of raising finance through cryptographic assets. Investors buy into the ICO and receive tokens in exchange.

When an entity raises funds in this way, it will record the receipt of an asset as the debit entry.

Possibilities for the credit entry include:

- **A financial liability** if the reporting entity is contractually obliged to deliver cash or another financial asset to the token recipient.
- **Equity** if the token recipient may be entitled to payments made out of distributable reserves but the reporting entity has no contractual obligation to deliver cash or another financial asset.
- **Revenue** if the recipient was a customer and a 'contract' (per IFRS 15 Revenue from Contracts with Customers) exists.
- **A provision** if there is a legal or constructive obligation to the token recipient.

Natural disasters

Some types of natural disaster, such as a floods, are becoming increasingly common. Natural disasters can have various financial reporting consequences.

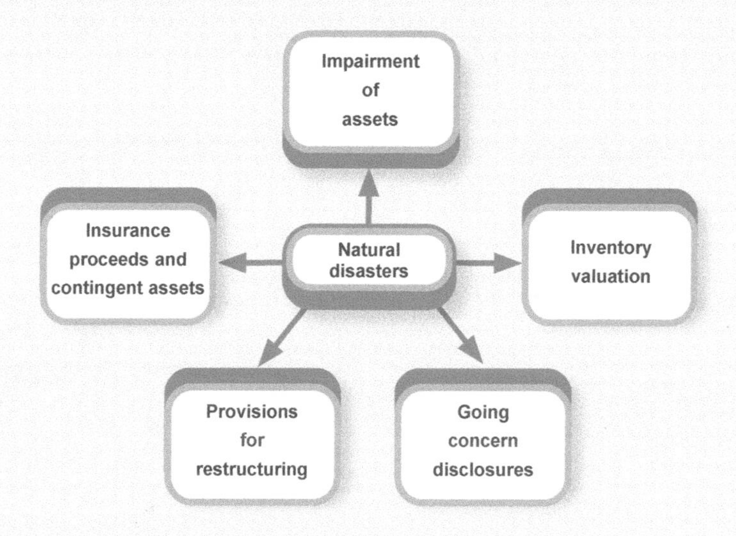

Materiality

Materiality is an important concept in financial reporting, but users and preparers of financial statements require more guidance on how to apply it. The Board has published guidance in a Practice Statement.

Definition

An item is material if omitting, misstating or obscuring it would influence the economic decisions of financial statement users.

Materiality judgements are required throughout the process of preparing financial statements:

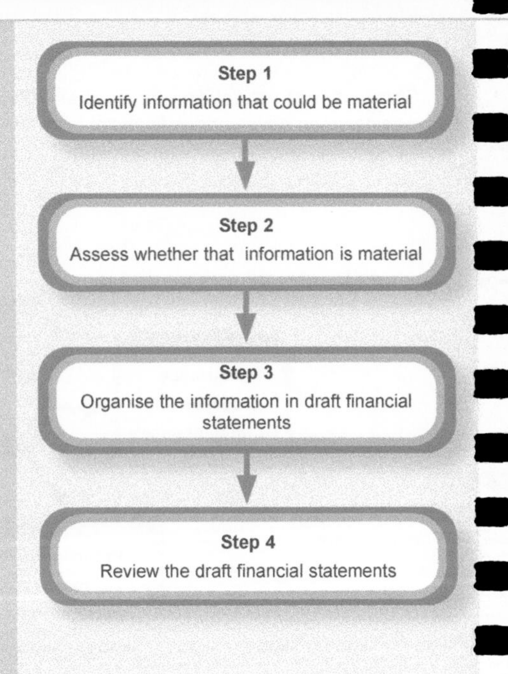

When assessing whether information is material, an entity should consider:

- Quantitative factors – measures of revenue, profit, assets, and cash flows
- Qualitative factors – related party transactions, unusual transactions, geography, and wider economic uncertainty.

An entity only needs to apply the recognition, measurement and disclosure criteria in an IFRS Standard when the effects are material.

Management commentary

Definition

Management commentary provides users with context through which to interpret the financial position, financial performance and cash flows of an entity.

Management commentary is not mandatory. However, the Board has produced a Practice Statement that provides guidance when producing management commentary.

Elements of management commentary

Management commentary should include information about:

- the nature of the business
- management's objectives and its strategies for meeting them
- the entity's resources, risks and relationships
- the results of operations and prospects, and
- key performance measures used by management to evaluate the entity's performance.

Developments in sustainability reporting

The problem

The IFRS Foundation has publicly recognised the importance of sustainability reporting for an entity's stakeholders. For example:

- **Investors** want more information about climate risks in order to inform their decision making.
- **Banks** are focussing on climate-related risks when assessing financial stability.

Many sets of sustainability standards already exist. This causes significant diversity in how entities report sustainability issues.

Proposals

The IFRS Foundation has proposed creating a new board, called the International Sustainability Standards Board (ISSB).

The ISSB would develop a global set of sustainability reporting standards with the aim of harmonising and streamlining reporting in this area.

Exam Focus

Exam Kit questions in this area:

- Carsoon
- Zedtech
- Holls
- Evolve
- Bismuth
- Symbal
- Colat

chapter

24

UK GAAP

In this chapter

- SBR UK.
- UK GAAP.
- Differences between IFRS Standards and FRS 102.
- Companies Act.

SBR UK

Exam Focus

This chapter is relevant for those who are taking the SBR UK paper.

UK GAAP

Guidance about the accounting standards that UK companies should apply is found within FRS 100 Application of Financial Reporting Requirements. The rules are as follows:

- Listed groups must prepare their accounts under IFRS.
  - However, the companies within the group can take advantage of disclosure exemptions outlined in FRS 101 when preparing their individual (non-consolidated) financial statements.
- Other UK companies will apply FRS 102 The Financial Reporting Standard Applicable in the UK and the Republic of Ireland unless:
  - they voluntarily choose to apply IFRS, or
  - they are a micro entity and choose to apply FRS 105 The Financial Reporting Standard Applicable to the Micro Entities Regime.

Differences between IFRS Standards and FRS 102

Some of the key examinable differences are summarised below:

	IFRS Standards	FRS 102
	Conceptual Framework	
Concepts	The Framework does not identify these as separate qualitative characteristics	FRS 102 identifies qualitative characteristics of materiality, substance over form and prudence.
	IAS 1 Presentation of Financial Statements	
Formats	IAS 1 provides recommended formats.	FRS 102 prepared in accordance with Companies Act 2006, therefore prescribed format.
	IAS 20 Accounting for Government Grants and Disclosure of Government Assistance	
Capital grants	Choice of using either the deferred income or netting off method.	FRS 102 prescribes the deferred income method only.

	IFRS Standards	FRS 102
	IAS 23 Borrowing Costs	
Borrowing costs	Eligible borrowing costs must be capitalised.	There is a choice to capitalise or expense borrowing costs.
	IAS 12 Income Taxes	
Deferred tax	Conceptualises deferred tax through the statement of financial position.	Conceptualises deferred tax through the statement of profit or loss.
	IAS 24 Related Party Disclosures	
Key management personnel	The disclosure of key management personnel compensation must be disaggregated e.g. short-term benefits, post-employment benefits, and share-based payments.	Key management personnel compensation is disclosed in total only.
Specific FRS 102 exemptions	n/a	Transactions between two or more members of a group need not be disclosed as long as any subsidiary is wholly owned.

	IFRS Standards	FRS 102
	IAS 28 Investments in Associates and Joint Ventures	
Goodwill (GW)	Goodwill arising on an associate is included within its carrying amount and is not amortised.	Implicit GW arising on an associate should be amortised.
	IAS 38 Intangible Assets	
Development costs	When the criteria are met, development costs must be capitalised.	There is a choice to capitalise or expense development costs.
Useful lives of intangibles	Intangibles can have an indefinite useful economic life.	All intangibles have a finite useful economic life, with a rebuttable presumption that this does not exceed 10 years.
	IFRS 3 Business Combinations	
Goodwill (GW)	GW is not amortised.	GW is amortised over its useful economic life.
	Gain on bargain purchase is recognised in profit or loss.	Negative GW is shown as a negative asset on the face of the SFP.

	IFRS Standards	FRS 102
Acquisition costs	Acquisition costs are expensed to the P&L.	Acquisition costs are added to consideration in goodwill calculation.
Contingent consideration	Include continent consideration in goodwill calculation at fair value.	If probable then include estimated amount of contingent consideration payable in goodwill calculation.
NCI	Choice of fair value method or proportionate method.	Only the proportionate method is allowed.
	IFRS 5 Non-current Assets Held for Sale and Discontinued Operations	
Discontinued operations	Discontinued operations are shown as one line on the P&L, with further detail provided in the notes to the financial statements.	Discontinued operations are shown in a separate column in the income statement.
Assets held for sale	When criteria are met, held for sale assets are presented as current and depreciation ceases.	No 'held for sale' category exists, so assets continue to be depreciated up until disposal.

Companies Act

Single entity financial statements

A company is exempt from the requirement to prepare individual accounts for a financial year if:

- it is itself a subsidiary undertaking
- it has been dormant throughout the whole of that year, and
- its parent undertaking is established under the law of an EEA State.

Group financial statements

A company subject to the small companies' regime may prepare group accounts for the year.

If not subject to the small companies' regime, a parent company must prepare group accounts for the year unless one of the following applies:

- A company is exempt from the requirement to prepare group accounts if it is itself a wholly owned subsidiary of a parent undertaking.
- A parent company is exempt from the requirement to prepare group accounts if, under section 405 of Companies Act, all of its subsidiary undertakings could be excluded from consolidation.

A subsidiary undertaking may be excluded from consolidation where:

- severe longterm restrictions substantially hinder the exercise of the rights of the parent company over the assets or management of that undertaking
- the information necessary for the preparation of group accounts cannot be obtained without disproportionate expense or undue delay
- the interest of the parent company is held exclusively with a view to subsequent resale.

Exam Focus

From the UK GAAP section of the Exam Kit, attempt the following questions:

- Leria
- Digiwire
- Crypto
- Fill
- Skizer
- Stem
- Sitka

References

This document references IFRS Standards and IAS Standards, which are authored by the International Accounting Standards Board (the Board), and published in the 2021 IFRS Standards Red Book.

The Board (2021) *Conceptual Framework for Financial Reporting.* London: IFRS Foundation.

The Board (2021) IAS 1 *Presentation of Financial Statements.* London: IFRS Foundation.

The Board (2021) IAS 2 *Inventories.* London: IFRS Foundation.

The Board (2021) IAS 7 *Statement of Cash Flows.* London: IFRS Foundation.

The Board (2021) IAS 8 *Accounting Policies, Changes in Accounting Estimates and Errors.* London: IFRS Foundation.

The Board (2021) IAS 10 *Events after the Reporting Period.* London: IFRS Foundation.

The Board (2021) IAS 12 *Income Taxes.* London: IFRS Foundation.

The Board (2021) IAS 16 *Property, Plant and Equipment.* London: IFRS Foundation.

The Board (2021) IAS 19 *Employee Benefits.* London: IFRS Foundation.

The Board (2021) IAS 20 *Accounting for Government Grants and Disclosure of Government Assistance.* London: IFRS Foundation.

The Board (2021) IAS 21 *The Effects of Changes in Foreign Exchange Rates.* London: IFRS Foundation.

The Board (2021) IAS 23 *Borrowing Costs.* London: IFRS Foundation.

The Board (2021) IAS 24 *Related Party Disclosures.* London: IFRS Foundation.

The Board (2021) IAS 27 *Separate Financial Statements.* London: IFRS Foundation.

The Board (2021) IAS 28 *Investments in Associates and Joint Ventures.* London: IFRS Foundation.

The Board (2021) *IAS 32 Financial Instruments: Presentation.* London: IFRS Foundation.

The Board (2021) IAS 33 *Earnings per Share.* London: IFRS Foundation.

The Board (2021) IAS 34 *Interim Financial Reporting.* London: IFRS Foundation.

The Board (2021) IAS 36 *Impairment of Assets.* London: IFRS Foundation.

The Board (2021) IAS 37 *Provisions, Contingent Liabilities and Contingent Assets.* London: IFRS Foundation.

The Board (2021) IAS 38 *Intangible Assets.* London: IFRS Foundation.

The Board (2021) IAS 40 *Investment Property.* London: IFRS Foundation.

The Board (2021) IAS 41 *Agriculture.* London: IFRS Foundation.

The Board (2021) IFRS 1 *First-time Adoption of International Financial Reporting Standards.* London: IFRS Foundation.

The Board (2021) IFRS 2 *Share-based Payment.* London: IFRS Foundation.

The Board (2021) IFRS 3 *Business Combinations.* London: IFRS Foundation.

The Board (2021) IFRS 5 *Non-current Assets Held for Sale and Discontinued Operations.* London: IFRS Foundation.

The Board (2021) IFRS 7 *Financial Instruments: Disclosure.* London: IFRS Foundation.

The Board (2021) IFRS 8 *Operating Segments.* London: IFRS Foundation.

The Board (2021) IFRS 9 *Financial Instruments.* London: IFRS Foundation.

The Board (2021) IFRS 10 *Consolidated Financial Statements.* London: IFRS Foundation.

The Board (2021) IFRS 11 *Joint Arrangements.* London: IFRS Foundation.

The Board (2021) IFRS 12 *Disclosure of Interests in Other Entities.* London: IFRS Foundation.

The Board (2021) IFRS 13 *Fair Value Measurement.* London: IFRS Foundation.

The Board (2021) IFRS 15 *Revenue from Contracts with Customers.* London: IFRS Foundation.

The Board (2021) IFRS 16 *Leases.* London: IFRS Foundation.

The Board (2015) IFRS for *SMEs Standard.* London: IFRS Foundation.

The Board (2021) IFRS Practice Statement: *Management Commentary.* London: IFRS Foundation.

The Board (2021) IFRS Practice Statement: *Making Materiality Judgements.* London: IFRS Foundation.

Index

A

ACCA Code of Ethics 11
Accounting policies 19
Acquisition date 116
Additional performance measures 151
Adoption of IFRS Standards 105
Agent 26
Agricultural produce 42
Amortised cost 77, 81
Analysis and Interpretation 147
Asset 3
Asset ceiling 57
Associates 125

B

Basic EPS 150
Biological asset 42
Borrowing costs 33
Business 115

C

Cash equivalents 142
Cash flow hedge 87
Cash-generating units (CGU) 37
Cash-settled share-based payments 67
Companies Act 175
Compound financial instruments 78
Concentration test 115
Conceptual Framework for Financial Reporting 2
Contingent asset 70
Contingent liability 70
Contract 25
Control 114
Control to control 133
Credit loss 83
Cryptocurrency 159
Current asset 16
Current issues 157
Current liability 17
Current service cost 58
Current tax 90
Current value 5
Curtailment 58

D

Date of transition 104
Deferred tax 90
Defined benefit 56
Defined contribution 56
Depreciation 31
Derecognition 4
Derecognition of financial instruments 84
Derivatives 85
Development 34
Diluted EPS 150
Direct method 144
Disclosure notes 17
Discontinued operation 20
Discontinuing hedge accounting 88
Disposal of overseas subsidiaries 139
Disposal of subsidiaries 131

E

Earnings per share 150
Economic resource 3
Elements 3
Equity 3
Equity instrument 76
Equity method 125
Equity-settled share-based payments 65
Ethical codes of conduct 11
Events after the reporting period 73
Expenses 3

F

Fair value 6, 117
Fair value hedge 87
Fair value hierarchy 6
Fair value through other comprehensive income 80, 81
Fair value through profit or loss 77, 80, 81
Finance lease 51
Financial asset 76, 79
Financial asset impairments 83
Financial instruments 75
Financial liability 76, 77
Financial performance measures 149
Foreign operations 139
Foreign subsidaries 136
FRS 102 169
Functional currency 44

G

Goodwill impairment 117
Grant date 65
Grants 32
Group cash flow statements 141

H

Hedge accounting 85
Held for sale 38
Highest and best use 7
Historical cost 5

I

IAS 2 Inventories 42
IAS 7 Statement of cash flow 142
IAS 8 Accounting policies, changes in accounting estimates and errors 19
IAS 10 Events after the reporting period 73
IAS 12 Income taxes 90
IAS 16 Property, plant and equipment 30
IAS 19 Employee benefits 56
IAS 20 Accounting for government grants and disclosure of government assistance 32
IAS 21 The effects of changes in foreign exchange rates 44
IAS 23 Borrowing costs 33
IAS 24 Related party disclosures 100
IAS 27 Separate financial statements 127
IAS 28 Accounting for Associates and Joint Ventures 125
IAS 33 Earnings per Share 150
IAS 34 Interim Financial Reporting 22
IAS 36 Impairment of assets 35
IAS 37 Provisions, contingent liabilities and contingent assets 70
IAS 38 Intangible Assets 34
IAS 40 Investment property 33
IAS 41 Agriculture 42
IFRS 1 First time adoption of IFRS 104
IFRS 2 Share-based payment 64
IFRS 3 Business Combinations 115
IFRS 5 Non-current assets held for sale and discontinued operations 20

IFRS 7 Financial Instruments: Disclosures 88
IFRS 8 Operating segments 96
IFRS 10 Consolidated Financial Statements 114
IFRS 11 Joint arrangements 126
IFRS 12 Disclosure of Interests in Other Entities 127
IFRS 13 Fair value measurement 6
IFRS 15 Revenue from Contracts with Customers 24
IFRS 16 Leases 48
Impairment 35
Income 3
Indicators of impairment 37
Indirect method 144
Intangible asset 34
Integrated reporting 153
Interim period 22
Investment property 33
Investments in equity 80

J

Joint arrangements 126
Joint control 126
Joint operation 126
Joint venture 126

L

Leases 47
Lessee accounting 49
Lessor accounting 51
Liability 3

M

Management commentary 164
Materiality 162
Measurement 5
Monetary 45
Most advantageous market 7

N

Net interest component 59
Net realisable value 42
Non-controlling interest 117
Non-financial information 152
Non-monetary 45

O

Operating lease 51
Operating segment 96
Other comprehensive income 5, 17
Other long-term benefits 61

P

Parent 114
Past service cost 58
Pension 56
Performance obligations 25
Presentation of financial instruments 76
Principal 26
Principal market 7
Professional ethics 10
Property, plant and equipment 30
Provision 70

Q

Qualitative characteristics 2
Qualitative characteristics of useful financial information 3

R

Recognition 4
Recoverable amount 36
Related parties 100
Related party disclosures 102
Remeasurement component 59
Research 34
Revaluation of PPE 31
Revenue 24

S

Sale and leaseback 53
Segment reporting 95
Settlement 59
Share-based payment 64
Short-term benefits 61
Significant influence 125
Small and medium sized entities 108
Statement of cash flows 142
Step acquisition 130
Subsidiary 114
Sustainability reporting 165

T

Tax 89
Temporary difference 90
Termination benefits 61
The acquisition method 116
The Conceptual Framework 2
The IFRS for SMEs Standard 108
Transaction price 26

U

UK GAAP 168
Unused tax losses 92
User groups 148

V

Vesting date 65